"CHOW SOLDIERS"

Wherever a fascist conqueror has tried to stand, the people have risen under his feet as guerrillas. That's the human race for you, and the Filipino people take their place big in it, just as big as the biggest.

AMERICAN GUERRILLA IN THE PHILIPPINES

THE BANTAM WAR BOOK SERIES

This is a series of books about a world on fire.

These carefully chosen volumes cover the full dramatic sweep of World War II. Many are eyewitness accounts by the men who fought in this global conflict in which the future of the civilized world hung in balance. Fighter pilots, tank commanders and infantry commanders, among others, recount exploits of individual courage in the midst of the large-scale terrors of war. They present portraits of brave men and true stories of gallantry and cowardice in action, moving sagas of survival and tragedies of untimely death. Some of the stories are told from the enemy viewpoint to give the reader an immediate sense of the incredible life and death struggle of both sides of the battle.

Through these books we begin to discover what it was like to be there, a participant in an epic war for freedom..

Each of the books in the Bantam War Book series contains illustrations specially commissioned for each title to give the reader a deeper understanding of the roles played by the men and machines of World War II.

AMERICAN
GUERRILLA
IN THE
PHILIPPINES

IRA WOLFERT

AMERICAN GUERRILLA IN THE PHILIPPINES
*A Bantam Book / published by arrangement with
the author*

PRINTING HISTORY
*Originally published by Simon & Schuster in 1945
Bantam edition / October 1980*

*Illustrations by Greg Beecham, Tom Beecham and
M. Stephen Bach.*

Maps by Alan McKnight.

*Bantam Books are published by Bantam Books, Inc. Its trade-
mark, consisting of the words "Bantam Books" and the por-
trayal of a bantam, is Registered in U.S. Patent and Trademark
Office and in other countries. Marca Registrada. Bantam
Books, Inc., 666 Fifth Avenue, New York, New York 10103.*

A FOREWORD

There were, I found, all sorts of ways to tell this story. The facts are these: Iliff David Richardson went out to the Philippines about a year before the war as an officer on the U.S.S. *Bittern*, a mine sweeper. He then transferred to the famous "expendable" motor torpedo boat Squadron 3, commanded by John D. Bulkeley, and fought these boats until they were shot out from under him. Then he involved himself in the guerrilla movement on Leyte, worked up to chief of staff to Col. Ruperto Kangleon, and ultimately became primarily responsible for the radio network which was General MacArthur's light back to Leyte.

One writer could have seen the boy who lived this story as an adventurer, one of that odd breed who is willing to do anything so long as it involves a restless and informal life. We used to call them soldiers of fortune, but since fortunes have become so hard to accumulate we call them, nowadays, adventurers. But the boy himself did not seem to fit. He wants to settle down when the war is over to a life of an academic nature. Nor does he fit as a man who fought the way he did because he is passionate in his politics. Like most Americans, Richardson's politics are the politics of a child. He wants things in his life to be as nice as they can be. When they aren't, he wants to know the reasons, and if he doesn't like the reasons he'll fight. This is not the stuff of great, selfless political heroes. Then there is a considerable affair of love involved. Richardson became attached to a very splendid girl, and, as opportunity after opportunity arose for him to escape from his dangerous guerrilla work, he thought up reason after reason for remaining with it and near her. It was easy to see a case of a man who thought—as some few in past and present times have actually thought—the world well lost for love.

However, in the end I decided the best thing was not to "interpret" or "edit" the story, but merely to set down its facts in as nearly true a way as could be. In that way the story could become larger than the story of Richardson himself—fascinating though that may be—and more important because it would be, instead of a story which fits an adventurer or a hero of politics or a love affair, a story of the whole guerrilla movement. I wanted very much to tell this story because I was surprised and delighted to discover how closely the untutored and relatively primitive guerrillas who fought the Japanese conquerors in the Philippines resembled the politically mature guerrillas whom I had met fighting the German conquerors in France and Belgium.

So here are the facts of the story, but before we start I think it ought to be recorded that Richardson was born in Denver on April 9, 1918, to a Methodist minister and his schoolteacher wife. His brother died before he was born, and he was the only other child. His father died before he was four, and his mother moved from job to job in town after town wherever people needed a teacher of Latin, history, music, or English. This went on for eleven years in Leadville and Lamar and through the sugar-beet country, and young Iliff lived from town to town and on his grandfather's cattle ranch near Springview, Nebraska, learning mostly how to live alone without being lonely, and how to create his own environment out of himself.

Children learn, if they ever do manage to, how to stand up to the best that is in them by the environment in which they grow up. They learn to depend on this environment more than they know. Throughout their lives most people live not so much as themselves but as reflections of whatever environment circumstances or their "fate" compel them to live in. When their environment becomes their enemy, it is able to beat them down, and in the separate-seeming, far-off-seeming, torpid, slow-breathing life of the jungles and barrios of the Philippines they become "bamboo Americans." But young Iliff, moving from town to town by the side of his schoolma'am mom, living year after year as "the new boy on the block," learned how to make himself his own environment and how, whatever the social climate, to stand up to the best in him.

After eleven years of this kind of instruction, the little family came into some money from the death of Mrs. Richardson's cattle-owning father and settled in Los Angeles, and Iliff grew up there from then on.

At twenty-six he has become a rather slight man of middling height, large-headed and with a somewhat pretty-looking face. He has brown hair, not light or dark, but plainly and truly brown. The skin of his face has a creamy texture, and the pink of youth is still on it. His eyes are large enough and his smile big and hearty and energetic enough to soften up the harsh strength in his face. However, the strength emerges. When this happens, it becomes clear that his eyes, his smile, and the creamy pink color of him are the only things soft about him.

If you—as the writer of him—try to find out what's inside him that made him do what he did, come to the Philippines as the sweet boy graduate of American schooling and manage to live successfully among ripe cutthroats and desperate, reckless, murderously passionate men and the whole fantastic melange of a guerrilla crew, if you try this you come up immediately against his belief in himself. He's not a genius or neurotic. Nor is he a man with extraordinary drive or with anything to him extraordinary at all, but just someone who seems to feel unshakably sure he can handle whatever he comes up against and not get hurt trying. He thinks he can do what he has to do, whatever it is, to get out of life pretty much what he wants, whatever that happens to be at the moment, and he moves along like that, solidly, his pride sitting in him like an anvil.

This belief in himself is not aggressive. It just sits there. It doesn't force itself on your attention, but just sits inside him stolidly and solidly. For example, he is the only one of the thousands of targets I have met in the shooting part of the present war to whom it has never occurred, under any circumstances, that he could be killed. Usually, there are three phases in the thinking of a human target. The first is "What the hell," and is compounded of the defensive belief that while a lot of people are bound to be killed, it cannot of course happen to you. The second phase is when your defenses have been knocked down and you realize how easily it can happen to you and you take the knowledge into your mind and understand it entirely and perfectly in each one of its separate, terrible, and very complicated meanings. There are many thousands of targets who never get past this phase, but stop their minds there and live there until they are dead or wounded or neurotic. But some, quite a considerable few strong-minded men, go on to the third phase, which is "What the hell" again, only compounded this time of belief in what the words actually say—that there is nothing to be done about it, so what the hell.

Richardson never got past the first phase. His defenses never were knocked down. It's incredible in a man who was a target for nearly three years of days and nights and who outlived so many hundreds of his friends and acquaintances and so many thousands of his enemies. But that's the fact of it. The knowledge that he could be killed knocked steadily at him, but it never gained admission into him, and all it got from knocking was sparks. The bullets and shells of the Japs couldn't do it. All they drew was sparks. The jungle and loneliness and defeat and impotence, falling on him, mouthing him with fungus-soft decay—they drew sparks, too. And when he cried into himself or those he loved cried against him, the splash of the tears drew sparks.

Oh yes, it's very clear, he's got this belief in himself and it sits in him like an anvil.

It will be noticed that some of those in this story are described solely by name. That is because Richardson could not remember clearly what they looked like. The author realized this lack may produce passing irritation and perhaps in some cases confusion for the reader. But he preferred to risk it rather than leave out anyone who shared in the making of a fine page in the history of our generation. The names are there—frequently with the spelling only guessed at—for the record and for the benefit of those who seek to know what perhaps the last work of their relatives was.

I.W.

AMERICAN
GUERRILLA
IN THE
PHILIPPINES

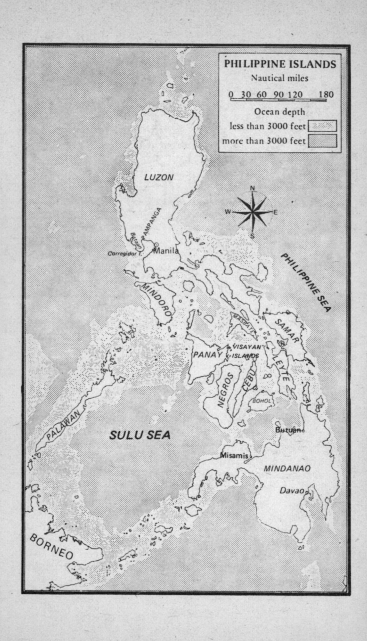

1

The thing was, said Richardson, we were living in a powerful steel and concrete world in the Philippines. Then the Japs kicked it out from under each one of us separately, piece by piece. They kicked or butted it out from under, or swamped it down by sheer weight, or trampled over it, or blew it up, or sneaked it out from under with their fifth columnists. The part of the world I was standing on at the time was one of those expendable mosquito boats that were written about. The Japs swatted at it pretty steadily from December 8 on, but it took them just four months and a day, until April 9, to shoot it away, and the way that happened was this:

However, if you don't mind, I'd like to go back to the day before that to tell you how we got to where we were when they knocked us personally out of the war. I don't like it thought that we were just sitting around waiting for them to knock us around.

Well, on this day, the day before our personal, non-negotiated armistice, a Jap heavy cruiser and destroyer were reported steaming slowly southward along the west coast of Cebu Island. We still had something of an organization functioning there, and our outposts called position, course, and speed on them on through the Tañon Strait between Cebu and Negros.

The warships were being very cheeky. They were making only eight knots, sauntering along like the bully of the block and his toady buddy looking for what was fit to spoil. Things had got like that by April 8. The Japs had thrown us pretty well into the street, and big and little bullets could roam around pretty much at will.

Our squadron leader, John Bulkeley, got out the

charts and figured if he was running the Jap ships he'd take them down to the southern tip of Cebu Island and put them in the channel there just north of Siquijor Island, where he would be able to intercept anything going or coming from the islands of Cebu, Negros, and Bohol. After that, Bulkeley sent to round up the liberty party.

PT Boat

They found me at the Macassar Bar all cozy in a nest of rum and cokes. This had been my first liberty since the war. I had been ringing that liberty bell steadily since the night before with all my might and patience, and I remember when I went out of the bar and down to the war again my brain was all full of noise and smoke and fumes and it felt like noise and fumy smoke curling and jittering through my blood. We were in Cebu City on Cebu at the time with the PT-34, on which I was executive officer, just out of drydock.

Dad Cleland ran the drydock there. He was manager of the Opan Shipbuilding and Slipway Corporation, a real fine old papa of a man. We had come in to him looking pretty sad from a beating we took. Our struts and shafts were really swoopsy. They went this way, you know, up and down, like a warble on a sound track, and the propellers were worse. Dad gave his Filipino boys a ten-pound hammer and some baling wire and a pair of pliers.

"My God!" I said. I was used to the big fine calibrating instruments and precision tools and machines of a United States Navy Yard and the very careful expert craftsmanship you get there.

But Dad said to leave his boys alone, they had done all right with worse. I couldn't take my eyes off them. I had never seen anything like that before. They'd line up a shaft which had to be exactly 100 per cent true and straight by sticking a piece of baling wire through it and squinting along it. Then one would say to the boy with the hammer: "Give her a couple of whacks on this side." Then squint again: "Whack her just a leedle leedle tape two or three times." It certainly seemed to me then the navy had gone a long way in my time, all of it downhill.

Well, we got the camouflage off in five minutes by making it an "all hands" chore. The camouflage was something we had thought up ourselves. Dad had built us a framework of timber to fit over the bow and make the boat look square-ended like a barge, and the rest of the deck, torpedo tubes, and canopy were covered with palm leaves and gunny sacks. The *Thirty-Four* came out of all that looking glad to be free and went pouring out of the harbor, the *Forty-One* boat with Bulkeley in command as guide. The *Thirty-Four* ran sweet as syrup. There was no vibration in her at all. Her bottom was clean. The power went smooth and true along the shafts, and the struts were firm, and the propellers bit clean into and through the water like the teeth of a powerful horse. You could see the whole thing on the tachometer repeaters on the engines. It was on the dial like a beautiful picture, the speed we were making. I tell you, if we'd only given Dad's boys two ten-pound hammers they'd have built us an extra boat.

When we got under way good, Bob Kelly, who was my skipper, told me, "Crap out, boy, you look like you need it." He knew I had been up all night. I went below and lay listening a minute to feel how sweet the boat was running. I put my hand on the bulkhead. I could hardly feel anything except the rum smoking in my hand. The *Thirty-Four* was creaming like a yacht. A PT boat usually runs like a nervous horse with a trembling all over and the muscles seeming to bulge out into you as you ride it. But old Dad and his boys had given us back a mahogany-seeming rubber mat of a yacht, and I remember very clearly the sound of the engines that day running soft and fast through my head while I lay there, and fresh, like a brook. The sound of the engines seemed to roll back the smoke standing up out of my blood from the rum in it, and I fell asleep with the feeling of rum smoke dispersing in me.

Then Kelly stuck his head down towards the forward compartment and called, "General quarters, all hands." Anyway, I think he did, because something woke me up and got me into the cockpit and on the wheel before I rightly knew that I still wasn't corked off in my sack. It was black night, five minutes after midnight the morning of April 9, 1942. I took the steering wheel alongside Kelly's battle station in these actions because if he was knocked out, why, there I would be, ready to take over without any waste motion. The *Forty-One* was seventy-five yards away on our port bow. Bohol Island lay inked in under the black night on our left, and Cebu and Negros were on the right. That put us in the center of the channel just north of Siquijor, where Bulkeley figured the Japs would go.

The blackness came out of my eyes slowly. I made out stars first, a lot of stars, and then the islands, and then I looked for the ships Bulkeley had figured on; and sure enough, just in the right place, was the biggest cruiser I had ever seen before. It was bearing 220 degrees true at a perfect target angle of 270 degrees. It was one of those heavy cruisers with the inverted-Y stacks, patrolling slowly about five thousand years off, and we were on it at the right time, too, at the time Bulkeley had figured on, with more than an hour and a half to play around in before the moon rose.

I'll tell you one thing about war: one of the handiest weapons to have is a commander who knows his business.

A light breeze was blowing. There was a little spindrift on the surface, row upon row of rifflings that we could step right up on and plane along when the time came for us to go. The night was very silent. The cruiser was slipping along silently. We all on board were silent, the little scufflings and slithers and drumpats of the men going to general quarters over now and everybody quiet now and tensed up ready to bang off a job of work. We idled up towards the cruiser, closing the range slowly at about twelve knots. A torpedo boat with throttles full open sounds like an airplane when it's changed the pitch of its propeller, and you can hear it five and ten and fifteen miles off. But when the three engines are idling, why, they just mutter along and you can't hear them for more than a mile or so, and we muttered along like that, that old thing you writers call battle fever climbing up me inside and running down me. It blew like a wind through the hairs of my legs. It puddled in the back of my head there and in my chest and in the back of my eyes, squeezing my eyes and puddling there, making me feel all dry and ragged inside. My heart was going in ragtime, and it was like I was walking around inside myself high and nervous and short-breathed and on tiptoe, straining to run but held back to a straining walk. That's the way it felt to me, all that.

Then ziiing-pung! The noise wasn't loud, but it clapped like a hammer against the inside of my ears. And ziiing-pung again. The *Forty-One* had fired two torpedoes. Right after that Bulkeley kicked over the *Forty-One*'s engines with full throttle. The sound of the engines went bursting over the night like a hill of rocks falling down a cliff. I don't know why Bulkeley did that, leaving us flapping there. He must have had a reason.

Well, Kelly jumped for our throttles. He threw them all the way forward and tightened the tension screw to keep them from working down to a lower speed from the vibration while Shepard (G.W. Shepard, MM 1/c), who had the watch in the engine room, wired the engines wide open. When you push the throttles as far as they will go, there is still about a sixty-fourth of an inch that can be held open with a wire to give you that little something extra, and Shepard sure gave it to us.

We were all working a mile a minute there then, with the *Forty-One* turning hard left and us barreling straight on in to close the range. But the Japs were clicking like sixty too. There was hardly any space of time at all between the roar of Bulkeley's motors and the Jap searchlight going on and sweeping over the *Forty-One* and stopping at us and fastening on our wake. There could not have been because I remember seeing in that first blinding glare the silhouette of Kelly looking sort of a bleached black as he leaned forward with the throttles and turned the tension screw. Then there was a flare of orange in the white of the searchlight, and in it, while the orange color of the Jap muzzle flash was still stuck in the air, there was a whistle overhead and the bang of their gun and a scooped-up crump from the shell exploding in the water behind us. They were all so close together that they came into the ear like one sound with three parts to it.

"Come right." Kelly spoke fast but soft. His voice was like a doctor's to a nurse when there's an operation on.

"Come right." I turned the wheel to bring the port .50-caliber turret to bear on the searchlight.

"Commence firing."

Reynolds (W. J. Reynolds, CC std) on the port turret didn't answer, just squeezed his itching fingers, and a whole barn door full of bullets flew in the direction of the searchlight.

But he was firing too low. We could see streams of his orange tracers plunging dotted lines into the darkness and pelting it and hitting the water and flinging high into the air in a ricochet. In a way it was lucky for us Reynolds was off, because the Japs probably figured we were firing at maximum range and falling short on that account. Anyway, they returned fire at maximum range and kept shooting over our heads. Then among the woodpecker chatterings of the cruiser's machine guns sounded the gobbling poomp-poomp-poomp-poomps of their Chicago pianos, the Bofors batteries, the orange-blue tracers of these coming in a straight line high over my head and then pulling down lower and lower and closer and closer while I kept lowering my head lower and lower under the bullets without realizing what I was doing until my chin burrowed so hard into my collarbone it hurt.

"Come left." Kelly was still talking fast and soft.

"Come left."

"Cease firing," he said to Reynolds.

He got no answer. The guns kept firing.

"The order is to cease that Goddamn firing," Kelly roared.

The guns cut off suddenly.

"Steady on the searchlight."

"Steady on the searchlight," I repeated.

The radio antenna mast forward was about four feet high. I turned it into the searchlight. It was like a gunsight. There was a metal brace on the windshield in front of me, and I lined that up with the antenna mast and the searchlight and made sure that way we were dead on the target.

We were busting right along all the time. The engines threw the boat to within one thousand yards of the cruiser. We went through the big wheee-bam scooped-up crumps of the heavy guns coming at us and the gobbling poomp-poomp-poomp-poomps of the Chicago pianos and then through a big white whole cloudy shimmering pine tree of water springing out of the sea two hundred yards dead ahead of us as a shell hit there, dimming the searchlight for a moment and giving my blistered-feeling eyes a chance to rest a moment. Then Kelly on the torpedo director fired the Number 4 torpedo.

"Right a touch."

"Right a touch."

I gave a little right rudder.

"Steady."

"Steady."

Then there was a noise the like of which I had never imagined existed. Goddamn if I ever heard of anything like that anywhere. I suppose nobody ever heard of it before because anybody who hears that noise generally dies in the midst of it. Generally he is blown up with the noise, but this time there was a freak and the shell passing eight or ten inches above my head had nothing to hit except the little oval radio mainmast which is due aft of the cockpit about forty or forty-two inches behind it. The shell hit the aluminum mast a couple of fingers' space below the yardarm used for signal hoists, and its forward motion was enough to propel it fifty yards astern of us before the delayed-action fuse took effect and she blew. Do you know what it was like? Do you know what the whole sound was like? I imagine you'd get a noise like that if you stuck your head inside the mouth of a roaring lion and the teeth crunched and you heard the roar of the lion and heard and felt the raking crunch of the teeth and heard and felt the bones and flesh of your head pulping and rending. That noise seemed like it just took me by the head and threw my head away with my body yanking after.

"Come right."

I heard Kelly yelling through all the ache and up-roar.

"Come right." I heard myself saying it through the boiler-factory banging in my head and fought back to the wheel like you fight up from under a boil of water although there was just air there between me and the wheel.

"Steady."

"Steady."

Then Kelly fired the Number 3 torpedo.

"Hard right," he bellowed.

"The rudder is hard right," I bellowed back.

I noticed then that all this time there had been sounds going on behind me, people saying things, and then I gathered Reynolds had been hit and the port turret was out of commission. But I didn't look around. I didn't dare. Our maneuver had fooled the cruiser's searchlight momentarily and we were out of the beam, but the light lunged after us like an animal and pounced on us and held us in its paws while the claws of the guns tried to rake us. We made a full circle about one hundred yards in diameter and then, under orders, broke out of the circle to bear down on the cruiser again at full speed.

Oh, momma, I told myself.

"Steady on the searchlight."

Momma, momma, here it is again, I said to myself.

"Steady on the searchlight," I repeated to Kelly.

Kelly wouldn't fire. We kept going full tilt, and Kelly wouldn't fire. There were match flares flickering all up and down the cruiser from the guns shooting at us. We were so close to them that I began to feel crazy. I guess Kelly felt crazy, too, because he wouldn't fire. I think maybe for a crazy moment there he wanted to ram that ship because there we were, already so close that I had to pull my head back and look up to see the cruiser's searchlight, and still he wouldn't fire.

Finally I couldn't stand it any more. "Mr. Kelly," I yelled, "we are going aboard."

But he didn't answer, just stood stock-still for another long crazy lifetime and then said, "Right a touch."

"Right a touch."

"Steady on."

"Steady on."

Then he let go the Number 1 and Number 2 torpedoes, beautiful new ones with great big beautiful warheads that we had swabbed lovingly with marfak and seen to that the pressure was okay on them, and they went gushing through the water, making the most wonderful bubbling little blurp of music anybody ever did hear.

"Hard right."

"The rudder is to the right," I yelled.

Let me tell you, it certainly was to the right. I nearly twisted the wheel off the socket. There are some wheelmen who like to work with the spokes, but personally I'm a handle man and I spun that handle right around to the peg and tried to push it through the peg the way you try sometimes when driving to push the gas pedal through the floor.

Then I noticed the destroyer there, the Jap destroyer. It had been shooting at us all the time but we had been too busy to notice. We couldn't miss seeing it now. The course we were taking led us right between the cruiser and the destroyer. But I was more interested in trying to watch the torpedoes go in. There is a grayish blue half-circle glare of lightning-vivid light that bolts out when a torpedo hits. It is the prettiest thing there is to see in the torpedo boat business. I had missed seeing our first torpedoes because we had started to circle when they had started to make their run, and now I missed the second two because of the angle we were at. When I looked back, all I saw were big black chunks of torn cruiser debris flying through the searchlight beam and making a rain of splashes in the water. I thought, it's the cruiser and destroyer firing at each other, all foozled up by our course change and the excitement there, and thought, well, anyway, we done that much, set them to knocking each other's brains out. But as we passed about two hundred yards astern of the cruiser, I saw the cruiser was dead in the water and I saw its searchlight begin to dim and then turn orange and then deepen into red and finally ruby red and finally glower out altogether, stone cold and black. Generator trouble will do that for a searchlight. Torpedoes chunking holes that let sea water in will give a cruiser generator trouble fast.

2

Anyway, our work was done for the night. We had no more torpedoes. We hauled tail the hell out of there. Our big white wake stood up high in the water and seemed just to blow furling out behind us like a scarf in a strong wind. Our course was south-southwest. The destroyer still lay between us and home. All we had left to throw at it was firecrackers, and we didn't have all the gasoline in the world and not all the room for maneuver either with a rocky, coral-littered shelf lying under the water from four islands around there.

We stuck to a course south-southwest until we got Reynolds patched up. He had taken shrapnel in the neck and shoulder, but he was comfortable and had not bled much and smoked a cigarette with pleasure. Then we altered course to the west and, when we saw the outline of Cebu, turned due north. We boiled along that way for quite a while, singing inside ourselves in that great singing feeling you get when an action's over and you've done all right in it. Then suddenly a searchlight banged on.

The searchlight didn't patsy around and sweep or poke here and there. It just banged on and clamped on our wake and clung there. And before we could get over our surprise, there was wheee-bam and the scooped-up crump of a shell exploding in water, the same sounds again, and again so close together that it was like one sound with three parts to it. It was the Jap destroyer. She was four, five hundred yards off. But there was some luck in the deal for us. She was proceeding due south at the time she passed us, and we were proceeding due north. That meant we were opening distance between us at a speed better than seventy knots.

14

I steered for the shell splashes. I had read about the Battle of Jutland and all the compensating the gunners there did for their misses and just hoped that those Japs of ours were on their toes the same way and would compensate like crazy every time they missed. So I threw the boat at whatever spot they had hit last, aiming for the shell splashes. Those Japs were all right. They were good, smart gunners. They compensated well and fast except for every now and then when some jerk there would be slow to think or would be just a jerk, and also, every once in a while, there would be one of those faulty shells that would skid and smack and hit the water tumbling and make an eerie string of blupping noises like you'd imagine one of those nonexistent sea monsters would make when it goes gulping after you to swallow you up. But we didn't get hit. We took no fragments or nothing, just two or three times a near miss that threw a sprayed-out wallop of water against the windshield so hard I thought it was shrapnel and ducked.

Finally, the destroyer gave up shooting at us and we straightened course. Then the moon came up at 0140. It was a very beautiful full moon. It made the sky look velvety and hung there like on a poster and softened us all up, and I remembered it was my birthday, my twenty-fourth. I didn't tell anybody. I just kept thinking about it. I wanted to fix the feeling of that birthday in my mind so that when I had my thirtieth birthday and fortieth and seventieth I could look back and remember how I had celebrated my twenty-fourth.

3

The entrance to Cebu City has Mactan Island on one side and Cebu on the other and is bordered by shoals. Navigation is further complicated by the fact that, particularly at night in wartime when everything is blacked out, there are no distinctive points there that can be used for fixes. When you've seen one part of the coast of Cebu Island, you've pretty much seen it all. It just runs on and on repeating itself.

Well, to make quite a long story short, we went into the wrong channel and ran aground on a jut of coral. It worried us. One past time when we had run aground close to shore, the Filipinos had taken us for Japs and shot holes into us. So I went ashore in the *Thirty-Four*'s punt to try to dig up a tug and, anyway, if that failed, to block off whatever shooting there might be with the morning sun. But by the time I got a telephone—at Minglanilia, the railroad station there—the tide had started to come in and the *Thirty-Four*'s crew had gone over the side and rocked her off the coral and taken off south in the direction where they thought Cebu lay.

It took Kelly time to figure out he was going wrong and back-track, and he didn't get into the approach to Cebu City until dawn. By then I was standing on Pier One with an ambulance, waiting for the *Thirty-Four* to tie up.

I could see the *Thirty-Four* working busily towards us. Then the air-raid alert sounded. Then I saw four Jap float planes coming in, looking for whatever had pickled their cruiser. I began to jump up and down. "Jesus," I said. "For Christ sake!" I ran back and forth a little way. There

16

was an army lieutenant standing there, a tall, powerfully built, middle-aged man. "What's the matter?" he asked, and I said, "Why, for Christ sake, they're going to get my boat and I'm not on it."

He knew the way I felt. I could tell he knew by the excited way he looked around to see what could be done about it. There wasn't anything to be done. But I liked him right away for the way he knew how I felt—Jim Cushing, a fellow about thirty-five years old who had been a wrestler once and then a chromium miner in the islands before joining the war.

The Japs came on in a "V." Then they peeled out of the "V" one by one to dive. They dove strafing and they dove right into the fire of the *Thirty-Four*. But torpedo boats in those days weren't what they are today, and we had only two twin-fifties on board and two lousy Lewis guns. The boys dished out what we had and the streams of tracers crossed each other in mid-air while I ran up and down, tearing at myself and letting little noises run out of my mouth. Then I saw the fat, yellow bomb coming out and saw the boat rigid under it, just held there flat and still-seeming. I groaned at the top of my voice.

Aichi E 13A "Jake"

17

Kelly was an iron-minded man, all right. He knew what he was doing. He didn't change course until the last possible splinter of a second so as to give the Jap no time at all to change aim. Then he flipped the boat over. The boat kicked to the right and the bomb hit the water near by on the port side.

I thought it had hit on the rail. That's the way it looked from where I was. The whole world stopped for me. White water stood up and hung there suspended. Smoke curled out of it while it stood there. The smoke curled like spumes of snow blown off a snow-smothered tree. Then the small, dark green *Thirty-Four* weaseled through, all motors roaring, and I shouted, "Missed! Missed! Goddamn, if he didn't make them miss," and looked full at Cushing and he grinned back at me with all his strength.

But—as I found out later—Harris (P. W. Harris, Torpedoman 2/c) on the port turret was already dead. He had been putting bullets smack into the Jap. The Jap had started to smoke. It couldn't gain altitude on the pull-out from its dive. (Later verified reports proved that one Jap plane crashed to the south and west of Cebu City.) "I got one," Harris yelled to Martino (J. Martino, CTM) on the starboard turret. "See it! See it! Did you see it?" turning his head as he yelled and following the plane from starboard to port with head high and neck stretched to receive the bomb splinter. The bomb splinter let him finish what he was saying. Then it went in right under his chin and drove up behind his face into the flesh of his brain.

Then there were more bombs and more strafings. One engine went out and then another. The starboard turret stopped working when Martino took a machine-gun bullet in the thigh. The Lewis gun forward stopped when Hunter (C. M. Hunter, CMM) had his upper arm broken by a bullet. One of a stream of bullets ripping open the canopy of the forward compartment like a can opener went into the groin of Reynolds, lying wounded below, and knocked up through his pelvis and bladder and intestines. The last gun on the boat went out of commission when a Jap bullet tore it right out of Ross's hands (W. L. Ross, QM 1/c), the bullet caroming off the gun and opening his thigh. And now Kelly was in trouble up to his neck and over that, up to his ears and the hairline of his forehead, with no guns left with which to fight back and only one engine with which to maneuver. I saw him sputter and wallow out of sight behind Kawit Island. Then he did not reappear.

I jumped into a car. I don't know how I got it. I was too excited. Cushing jumped in after me. He didn't have any reason. He just did, and we tore on down to Tanke, the nearest point of Kawit. We drove with hand on horn and foot pressing the gas pedal through the floorboard, the ambulance piling after us.

The airplanes had gone away. I ran down to the beach and got a baroto—a dugout canoe—there somehow, I don't remember, just took it, I suppose, and paddled with Cushing for the sound of the *Thirty-Four's* engine. We could still hear it going.

Then we saw the *Thirty-Four* aground behind one of those native bamboo fish traps. The flag was still there. It made me feel strange to see it flapping sluggishly in the breeze as if nothing had happened. I suppose your country is always like that. It goes on and on in its own way whatever happens to you, but it made me feel strange to see the flag flapping away in the same old way, and then I scrambled over the stern and I remember the engine blowing fumes in my face and my wrinkling my face up "whew!" and then there the whole thing was flat before me. A sieve, that's what it looked like, the deck there, a mangled-up sieve of bullet holes with blood dripping through them.

Kelly had got the wounded ashore on Kawit. They had lit out so fast they hadn't had time to shut off the one engine still working. They had left the dead behind. I found Harris lying quietly below where they had laid him, KIA, certainly that, oh absolutely that—KIA: Harris, Torpedoman 3d Class, United States Navy. I remember running topside after that, thinking who'd ever have thought Harris would be a KIA, and then seeing Kelly come wading back.

"Congratulations, Mr. Kelly," I said, on his being alive.

"Well," he said, "well..." and stumbled around a

19

little bit in his words, and then said, "Hell, I wasn't worried about me. Hell, they can't get me. I'm too tough."

I was so glad to see him I told him that was true, that was the absolute truth, and then we got busy floating the dead and the wounded ashore on the doors to the forward compartment.

Mrs. Charlotte Martin, an American who lived at Cebu with her husband, "Cap," was at the hospital helping. Reynolds became conscious on the operating table. "I'm going to be very sick, ain't I?" he said to her. That was the only thing he said.

"Oh no," she told him, "only for a little while."

Then she leaned forward to stroke his forehead and saw he was dead.

We tried to save the *Thirty-Four*. After all, Dad Cleland's boys still had their pair of pliers and ten-pound hammer. Lt. Tom Jurika made the inspection. There were two pilot boats for the party. There were a lot of Filipino soldiers to help and other people—including Jurika and Cushing. Then two Jap planes interrupted them with a sneak attack. They chopped off their engines and came gliding soundlessly out of the sun, then cut their engines back in with a Godawful grind and came on shooting.

They cut the Number Two pilot boat just about in half. Then they came back for the Number One boat. Everybody was trying to wade ashore. They were spread out in a rough line about forty-five feet long, all intent on getting ashore. There were about fifteen inches of water and four inches of slimy mud under it. You couldn't figure out whether it was faster to swim or wade. Then the explosive bullets came into the Number One boat behind. It sounded like two machine guns going at once—one from the plane, and the explosive bullets hitting sounded just like there was a machine gun working on the pilot boat.

Then the planes went for the men. They strafed the center of the line. Some tried to dive under the water. They saw the white-beaded line of bubbles from the bullets, but they couldn't stay under. They couldn't keep the water over them as a cover. There was too much positive buoyancy there because it was so shallow.

Incidentally, those who swam got to the beach faster than those who waded.

When the attack was over, there were two dead and there was a third fellow who had squeezed himself for safety in a small forward compartment in front of the cabin of the Number One boat. He had been clasping his knees and legs to fit himself in there. His back had been to the diving plane. A bullet hit him in the right shoulder, came out through a lower right rib, then went on through the thigh bone, coming out just above the knee, and after that had gone through the calf of his leg, breaking the shinbone on the way out. He had six holes in him and four major bones broken by the one bullet.

And the *Thirty-Four* was on fire. She was burning like a Christmas tree, hopelessly and beyond redemption. I didn't realize fully at the time what that meant to me. We are all members of a rich, young, energetic country. When an American gets knocked off his perch in a fight and his perch is splintered up under him, the first thing he thinks of is, hell, I'll get me another perch, that's the least of it.

But it isn't the least of it. No sir, it certainly is not.

4.

Kelly had put me in charge of the funerals. But we couldn't get anybody to officiate until the next morning. Then Tom Jurika said to come with him, he'd bed me down where there was chow enough and something extra to wash the war out of me. He had borrowed a fine penthouse apartment in the Heacock Building.

I was too tired to eat much. The radio was on. We tuned in our station on Corregidor and the news came over that Bataan had fallen. This was no Jap talking. This was our own people, but I was too tired to think about it and went to bed. I remember I sat on the edge of the bed to take my shoes off. They were wet and full of sand and muck. But I was too tired to unlace them and thought, I'll lift my feet up and unlace them that way. But I was too tired to lift my feet up and thought, if I lay down a minute maybe I'll get energy to unlace my shoes. So I lay out flat then and tried a little to get up and knew I'd never be able to get up and thought, I ought to pull the cover over me because a chill will come into my bones and wake me up. But I was too tired to reach out my hand to do it, and fell asleep even while I was thinking of doing it.

Explosions started about four-thirty in the morning. That was the army blowing up Cebu. The explosions woke me up. I was very cold. I lay drowsing through the explosions a long time wondering what they were. Then there was a very big one with a lot of glass crashing. It shook the building. I got up and wandered freezing through the apartment. It was empty. Jurika had gone. I went down into the street. The city was burning. There was an eerie light, red as watered blood.

I headed for the waterfront. I found Tom there. "The Japs are here," he said. I was stupid from all the feeling of excitement I had and looked past him out into the harbor. "No," he said, "they're landing about ten kilometers down. You can see them from Busay. We're burning the town for them."

You could look right up through the red air and see the black, quiet sky over it. There were sparks sailing there. They were big long sparks and they sailed like ships, crazily, like ships being pulled and turned and bounced in rapids.

I went with Tom to the army warehouse. It was a very big one. I remember walking around like on air. There was a crazy feeling in the air, and there was this crazy light and the sky hanging black and quiet over it, and it just felt when I walked that I had to fight my feet down through the crazy air to touch ground.

We had four five gallon tins of gasoline. We sprayed them around and touched a match and ran along, touching matches here and there and feeling crazy.

Then we went over to a big office building near the downtown American Club. I don't remember the name of it. It was a brand-new beautiful building. We brought gasoline with us. We started piling up everything in the center of the floor. We took out all the files we could find and threw them in a pile there, and the chairs and tables and desks, anything we could lift we threw in and slicked over with gasoline. Curtains. We tore down curtains and threw them in to make the fire better. Then the telephone rang. I felt just like a cop had come in. Tom answered. It was a Britisher whom we met later.

"I say," he said, "are you there?"

"Where?" asked Tom. "Are we where?" because neither of us was very sure where the hell we were. Then Tom yelled to me. " 'Is rile 'ighness wants to know are we where we is, or isn't we?"

"Not all of us," I said. "We are not all there."

I thought that was very funny at the time, and Tom did, too.

"Oh, it's just a bloody balls-up," the British said. "I'm at transportation and there is no transportation. A motorcar here and a beastly wade through fire to get here, and not a single motorcar in the whole bloody f—ing motor pool."

"Old top," cried Tom, "I jolly f—ing bloody well have to say cheerio now. This joint is on fire."

"Cheerio, old man, and all that," I shouted from where I was, and Tom tore the telephone loose and threw it on the pile in the center of the room.

Then we set the place on fire and ran around throwing chairs through the glass of the windows to make the draft better. It made us feel like kids letting loose.

After that we went back to the penthouse and got some cans of chow that Tom had. I still had my navy shoes on. They were all soggy and there was blood on them, too, from carrying the wounded. Tom gave me a pair of his shoes left over from civilian days, and we drove to Busay Heights in his car to see the Japs come in.

The heights were full of abandoned cars. People had driven them that far and then had decided it would be safer to walk. They didn't know where to go, but they felt it would be safer to walk. It was daytime now. The town lay burning below us. A thick cloud of smoke hunkered over it, and in it were orange- and lemon-colored bonfires from buildings burning, and over it were Jap airplanes, coasting like buzzards and looking for something to hit. There were eleven Jap vessels landing men down the coast. I could see them very plainly with my binoculars. There was no smoke there and no fire and the Japs were working with the easy speed of experienced troops at a drill.

Tom and I shot up the engines of the abandoned motorcars with our forty-fives and those we could we pushed over a cliff there. We drove his car over a cliff, too, like we had seen it done in the movies, jumping out just before the plunge to death. Then we went to Cap and Charlotte Martin's house, where we had a good view of the town and the Japs coming in. She broke out champagne and a fine dinner, although it was only a little past breakfast time for her.

We saw the Jap mine sweepers come into Cebu Harbor. Then more Jap ships pulled up to the three lovely docks there. There wasn't anything shooting at them. The

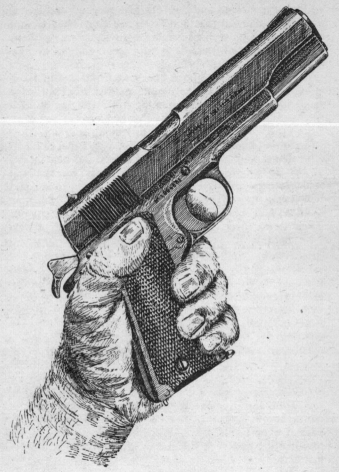

Colt .45 1911A1

army had no artillery to answer the ships' guns, just rifles and machine guns, so they fell back from the waterfront and dug in in the residential section of town after blowing up the industrial section. A wind sprang up from the sea and the city crackled under it. The fires reached up like red arms into the cloud that hung over the city. They twisted and seemed to be trying to pull the cloud down on them. The cloud was all shades. It was gray and white and gray-black and blue-black and brown-black and pure brown and pure blue. Smoke kept rising into it and leveling off in it. Some of the smoke poured like out of a funnel and was thick, mushrooming stuff, while some of it just rose quietly. The cloud yawed away from the red arms of the fires, circling slowly and then clotting down. Now and then there would be a big explosion and the cloud of multicolored smoke would flap in it slowly and heavily.

We were more than ten kilometers away, but the heat got us. It grew in the house and grew on our faces, and when I put my fingers on my hair I got a burning sensation. I kept thinking of what it must be like for our soldiers down there, stuck right into the heat and preparing to fight in it. We slept that night in Mrs. Martin's house. It was very hot all night from the fires. Cebu is the second largest city in the Philippine Islands. A red light danced all night in the darkness of the room where we slept. It played and lifted and fell and went back and forth across the ceiling and walls and floor and over our hands and faces. I put my arm across my eyes, but the red light came in under my arm.

5

There was a lot of walking for us after that. The Japs bombed and strafed the house the next morning, and we cut loose from it to look for the army and join the fight the best we could. People speak of the Jap flood. There was no flood of Japs. We were the flood. We were in it and we were it, while the Japs were just the rocks and walls sticking up that the flood flowed around. You couldn't seem to stand still. Whatever you stood on crumbled away and became part of the flood and set you drifting again.

You'd see buqwees, as they call the evacuees there, going north and south on the same road. There were long lines of families of them, none of them knowing where to go, but going, keeping on going. There were plenty of people losing their nerve. Americans lost their nerve just like anybody else. One time, Tom was sleeping on a cot jammed in close to another cot where there was another American officer. In the middle of the night, this fellow put his gun into his ear and blew his head all over Tom's blanket. It gave Tom a terrible ringing in his ear. It was so loud that even the next morning when he was burying this fellow he couldn't hear the dirt he was throwing into the grave.

We found a colonel, finally, sitting with a staff around him, and he put me in charge of his transportation. Tom went off to look for headquarters, and I stayed with the trucks and busses. I won't tell you the colonel's name. The chances are a hundred to one he's dead now and what's the use blackening the dead. But he was really worthless. He was plain no good. He'd close his lips tight, but even then you could hear his teeth knocking together behind them.

27

There were twenty trucks and busses, and my job was to use them to bring in all the supplies from the various bodegas* the army has scattered around the island. I never worked so hard in my life. I was glad to get something to work at after that feeling of being adrift and not going anywhere really, and I worked from five o'clock in the morning until eleven at night. I wasn't sure I was accomplishing anything, but at least it looked like something. It felt like work with sense to it. Then the Japs took Busay and started coming towards our motor pool. I got on the phone to the colonel's command post.

"The Japs are about a kilometer and a half away from here," I told him. "Do you want me to burn the trucks?"

"Are you sure?"

That's what he asked me, was I sure. "I saw them," I told him. "They were poking through one of the trucks that got bombed down there. I am sure I saw them and I am sure of the distance because of the truck."

The colonel was very excited. "I'll call you back," he said. I could hear his fear in the telephone.

There were a lot of Jap planes after that. They were really bombing on that day. They put a bomb into a moving truck and they worked all around the motor pool, putting a ring-around-a-rosy of bombs around it, doing it neatly to spare the trucks and supplies while at the same time chewing up any perimeter of defense. But the laugh was on them. We had no perimeter of defense, just us lying shaking in the holes. Every rifle was down on the line, wherever that was, and all I had for the trucks was Filipino boys and bare fists.

I kept sitting by the telephone. I had my cans of gasoline set up in a line along the line of trucks, waiting for the orders to scorch the earth. I was afraid to do it without orders. I knew our line was very thin and the Japs could go through it anywhere they really tried, but I thought maybe we were going to counterattack, maybe we were saving these trucks for a counterattack. I had lost some of my boys in the bombing, dead and wounded. I lost some more when they took off with the wounded to look

*Stores.

for a hospital. They didn't come back. There were some who just scattered under the bombing. They didn't come back either. They knew. They knew just as well as I did, but I sat by the telephone waiting.

The road to the motor pool from Busay was a curving one. It curved around a hillock about four hundred yards away from us and went off on a walk of its own before coming back to us. But, from the hillock on, the Japs didn't use the road. They came straight to the point that day, right over the hillock, and the first thing I noticed was the rest of my boys taking off and running like a flight of butterflies across the fields away from the hillock, twisting and fluttering and zigzagging. All except one. He stuck by me by the telephone.

Automatic rifle bursts came from the hillock. Why, I thought, they are about a minute and twenty seconds' fast walking away. I counted ten, waiting for the telephone to ring. It didn't, and I counted ten more. Then I gave it ten for good measure and waited another little while without counting. I saw the first Japs coming down the hillock and waited until they got to the bottom of it. Then I told the boy to take off at a tangent from the telephone.

"God run with you," I said.

"Oh, sir," he said, "God run with you."

I took off at another tangent, but while we were very close I saw him suddenly jump high into the air and saw he had no back any more to his head and saw him run a little way more with no back to his head, then fall. I kept on butterflying across the fields.

I went right in to the colonel. I didn't stand on any formality. He was a full colonel, but I just busted in and didn't wait to be spoken to. "The Japs got all the trucks on a platter while I was sitting waiting for you to call me up and give me orders," I told him.

"Are you sure?"

"Why, Goddammit," I cried, but he didn't wait for me to finish. He could tell I was sure about the Japs by how angry I was. He got up and walked past me and said to his adjutant, "We're taking off. Pass the word to wrap the camp up and take off." Then he went out, leaving me there without any orders or anything.

I could have followed him, but what was the use? He

was in the flood, too. Everything was. Nothing had anything to stand on. The Japs took the whole headquarters of General Chinowitz with a truck and three light tanks.

After that I walked some more and then I stayed in a cave for two days, one of those limestone caves like they have in Kentucky. I found two Americans living in it, and one of them gave me a razor. I think that's why I stayed and because I was tired. These two Americans were

Model 95 Light Tank

civilians, businessmen on the island. They didn't know what they were doing in the cave either. One of them was an oil man, middle-aged, a former marine. I forget his name, but I remember hearing he died later, trying to make it to Australia. The other fellow was quite an old boy. I guess he was in his fifties. His name was Wooster, or something like that, I don't remember exactly. I stayed there two days and two nights, and all I remember out of it is that, and the long line of buqwees going by in two directions on the road on top of the hill up above, the buqwees going east telling the others the Japs were to the west, and the buqwees going west telling the others the Japs were to the east, each side knowing the other was right but keeping on walking because they didn't know what else the hell to do. There were bats, too. I remember them, too. I remember lying in the cave all shaved and rested and waiting nice and quiet to fall asleep, and the bats flying in and out overhead—pfooot, pfooot, pfooot, in swift, fluttery rushes until I fell asleep.

Then I heard from the buqwees there was American Army two kilometers away and found them there hidden away in jungle, keeping themselves a secret from everything. Bill Hocking, a British friend of mine, was in that camp. He had just joined the army. They had a prisoner there, too, who was supposed to be the son of the late Admiral Yamamoto. He was a flier who had crashed. Nobody was guarding him. He was wandering around free on his promise not to escape. He was a big husky kid. Sometimes he would cry because he had been captured. He was sleeping with Hocking and he'd cry and tell Hocking he wanted to commit suicide. Finally, Hocking got tired of being waked up and cried over. "Brother," he said, "here is a gun. If you want, I will help you pull the trigger." But the Jap made believe he didn't understand. Then, when he couldn't keep that up any longer, he indicated he couldn't soil himself with anything less than ritual hara-kiri knives, of which we were in very short supply.

Hocking told him. He told him straight. This is the kind of a guy you are: when the time comes for you to die, you will be willing on condition that there is no other way out and St. Peter comes downstairs personally to take you by the hand and lead you into heaven. But if there was another way out, the deal would be off.

Hocking was quite a man, really quite that, a real hell of a swell guy, a big, handsome, happy man. He's dead now, and that whining Jap was turned back to his people when the camp there surrendered.

31

There wasn't much use to the camp there. They were just filling in the time until the Japs came up and took them. So a party of us decided to try to get on to Leyte and so perhaps make Mindanao and a plane to Australia. I had a priority from MacArthur. He had given it to all the PT people who had taken him out of Corregidor. We weren't supposed to use it until we had no more mosquito boats to fight off of. Well, that was the case now. There wasn't a PT boat left alive between the Balambana forest and Bayonne, New Jersey.

6

It's kind of mixed up now, the running to here and there of those days. It seems so long ago. Every time I realize it's only three years it's a shock to me, but I remember there was a party of us, army-navy, who got finally, walking, to Danao and then I could not go any farther. I could not walk another step, a lymph gland in my groin was swelled up so.

It was a very puzzling business. Nobody had ever heard of a lymph gland going haywire over too much walking. A doctor told me my mind did the whole thing. I was pushing my body around too much, so my mind gave my body something wrong with it to stop me. Well, that's not scientific. It's not the scientific way of saying it. It makes it sound like I have two wives and a mother-in-law on my mind. But it happened to me several times and I've seen it several other times in the jungle, that the mind can do this, lay you low with a physical ailment—with skin ulcers, for instance—just because you're pushing yourself to do what part of you does not really want to do. Me it laid low with a swollen lymph gland.

Ultimately we wound up in Tacloban on Leyte where Colonel Cornell's headquarters were. I was still hobbling. The headquarters were a place where the flood had jammed up. There was a regular driftwood jam there. Everybody from everywhere north and west and east, who had been drifting from point to point of the compass, stopped there and asked for something they needed or thought they needed or just wanted. They needed food or ammunition or clothes or medicines or money or gasoline or someone to wipe their nose for them and stood jamming

33

the place and arguing and protesting and begging and being indignant.

Then a girl came in with an elderly woman. I noticed her first, I think, because she was so quiet. Not the woman. I don't mean I noticed the woman particularly. The woman was just as quiet as the girl, but I noticed mostly how quiet the girl was. My eyes were starving in that place for something quiet to rest on and there she was, looking very fresh and relaxed and at ease and nice, just plain nice to look at. She was a girl about five feet four, a beautiful figure and classic features, with long wavy and curly hair, medium dark.

I let myself be jostled and edged over by the mob there until I was next to her. I wanted to smell her. That may sound funny, but after you live in your clothes long enough, you want to smell something fresh and sweet. You'd give anything to smell something that smells like a nice girl—you know what I mean, good clean lather-making soap, freshly laundered clothes, the dry sweet smell of cosmetics, and that sort of crinkly fragrance they've got in their hair. Why, if you can believe it, when you're in that condition even the sound of their laugh has a smell to it. It's a smell that's hard to describe—warm and mildly pungent, just a trace pungent but mostly dry warm, and when they give a nice laugh, you not only hear it but smell it, too. Anyway, I sniffed at Curly quite a while before I felt like trying to start up a conversation.

"These people all think they need something," I said to her suddenly, as if we had been talking together a long time, "but what they need first is a good, swift kick."

The elderly lady behind—her aunt, I found out later—stirred defensively. Those Spanish people are very strict. But Curly answered quickly, before her aunt could do anything about it, something to the effect that I please shouldn't try it until my foot got better.

We were off then. We were off the starting mark together and couldn't be turned back now whatever this chaperon of hers thought about our talking together without being introduced by her parents. Because I knew then Curly had noticed me the same as I had noticed her, else how could she have seen my hobbling.

I was so glad to learn she spoke English! This big relief I felt at learning that from her own mouth comes back to me now, while I am sitting here in New York, just as sharp as I felt it then in Tacloban. She spoke English with the cutest little Spanish accent. The words came out kind of dolled up, trimmed at the edges or with a little curl to them like each word had an aroma of spice to it and had just stepped out of a barbershop. Her English was perfect, except every now and then she would put a word in the wrong place, in the Spanish place. This happened mostly when she was tired. She wasn't wearing any hat, just a little skullcap, a calotte I think they call them, on the back of her head that you could hardly see with all the beautiful curly hair piled up in front. She was beautiful without smiling, but when she smiled it was just like the sun. Her face lit up and it looked so darn nice.

I know all this sounds like I'm giving you a whole crock of hock or something. But Curly is a wonderful person. I think if you just saw her pass by you would know she was outstanding in the world.

She was there to find a place in the hospital for her cousin's wife, Loling Escano, who was going to have a baby, and I was there to hook a ride down to Mindanao, so there didn't seem to be any chance we would ever meet again. But I certainly liked standing alongside her and talking to her that day.

I didn't meet Curly again until more than a week later. It was quite some week. I told them down in Mindanao I had this priority from General MacArthur to fly to Australia, and there was an army man there, a Captain MacGregor, who said to me I was exactly one day too late. The Japs had walked in on Del Monte the previous afternoon. All I was in time for, he told me, was the surrender. There was going to be a big party. They would all drink barbed wire.

"Is there an alternative?"

"Oh yes, if you don't like to drink barbed wire with us, you don't have to. A boy blowing in the way you did, unattached and everything, there is an alternative for you, which is to get off the island if you can."

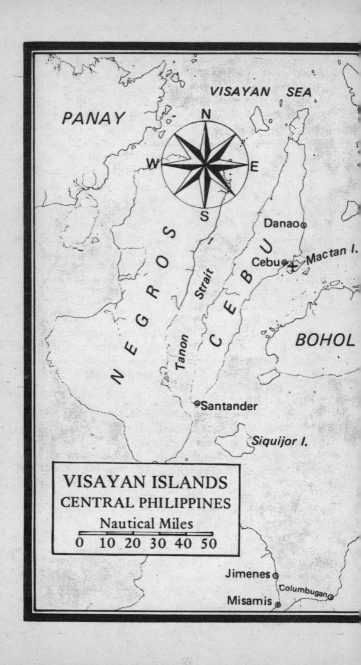

I remember MacGregor spoke in a very quiet and easy way. There was no rush about him or strain in him.

"The rest of us here," he said, "the people attached and under orders, why, we are all going to the party. We are getting ourselves a gun apiece and going down to the line and shoot our gun into the Japs until we're out of ammunition. Then we'll surrender. It is going to be some party. There will not be a desk in the army, not a damn thing to make out in triplicate, nothing to file, nothing to go through channels. The only channels will be the barrel of a gun." MacGregor seemed to enjoy the prospect. "Some of the fellows, I think, don't like the idea of living in a Jap prison anyway. They want to make this party their graduation exercise."

So I went back to Leyte on the same lugger I came in on. I took eleven unattached Americans with me. Ten of them were Air Corps enlisted men who had got away from Del Monte in a Wrigley Spearmint Gum wagon, and the eleventh boy was Pierson (E. E. Pierson, BM 2/c) whom I knew from the PT days. I remember the first time we were bombed, right after the war started, Pierson lost his head and jumped overboard. It was a silly thing to do because concussion from the bombs falling in the water is very bad and there are always more bombs falling in the water than on the target. But right after that, two or three days after that, this same boy who had lost his head saved our lives when we ran aground. The Filipinos on shore there, off the reef on which we ran aground, couldn't make out what we were. The red of the American flag didn't look like it was in stripes to them, but looked like the red of the Rising Sun of Japan from where they were. So they started putting rifle bullets into us. We all took up armor plate and got behind it, but Pierson grabbed up a white sheet and waded right into the bullets with it. They must have thought he was a one-man landing party or something because they turned a real hailstone barrage of small-arms fire on him. But he kept right on wading into the bullets and waving the sheet, and finally he cooled the guns off.

These eleven fellows had joined forces in wandering around trying to find a way to Australia. I told them to hook on to me, I had the same idea.

On the way back to Leyte we stopped at a small island. We were the first Americans the people there had seen since the invasion. They came to meet us with a regular gutter band, like the German bands that used to play in the streets back home, with plenty of oompah horns to them. Then later in the evening the band played at a dance they gave for us. We all felt just plain like hell when we saw the band and the people cheering because we thought they didn't know the score and believed we had come to save them. But they knew the score all right. They just wanted to show us they appreciated what the Americans had tried to do and wanted to indicate how glad they would be when the Americans came back. The general impression was they would keep a light in the window for the Americans to come back to. That was the first inkling I ever had the soil was ripe for a guerrilla movement.

By the time I got back to Colonel Cornell's headquarters at Tacloban, he had received a dispatch from General Sharpe. It was something to the effect that you are hereby released from my command, surrender is imminent.

"Boy," he told me, "if you stay with us, I'll have to surrender you with everybody else. That will be my orders, and where I fall down in the surrender agreement the Japs will fall down in their treatment of our fellows that they already have."

"And if I don't stay with you?"

"Well, I can't surrender what I haven't got, can I? How much money do you need?"

His till could stand a tap of two thousand pesos. That was a thousand dollars. I made sure to find a good sailboat, or what I thought was a good one. Finally I found a banca that seemed a beaut. It had been hewn out of a single terrific log. It was about forty feet long. On deck, it flared out somewhat to be three and a half feet wide, but at the waterline it was a foot narrower. Let's see, that gives her a length-to-beam ratio of about fifteen to one. Yes, I think that's about right. The thing I liked about her, she was single-masted. This was unusual for a banca that size. Usually when they were that big, they had two masts. With one mast we had a better chance to fool Jap patrol boats as to how important we really were. There was a triangular sail which, with the native rig, went much higher than the mast. The owners were very proud of the sail. They wanted 180 pesos for it and 120 pesos for the banca itself.

To show you what prices had become by that time, I paid 370 pesos for twenty-five pint cans of milk, $9.40 a pint, and for the lot more than for the whole banca and sail. But there were more people intending to stay in prison than light out for Australia, so the demand for canned milk was very brisk. Well, I bought the transportation on condition that they'd give me five experienced banca men to sail me back in it to Tacloban within an hour. I had never been on a sailboat before. None of us had. I wanted some idea of how the thing worked before taking off for the long run down under the world.

I got back to Colonel Cornell's headquarters about six-thirty in the morning. Sheets, jibs, booms, tillers, they were all flickering in my head as I slept. I was asleep about a half hour when the colonel woke me up to show me a dispatch from General Sharpe: "Cancel my NR 35," or whatever the particular number was. "You are hereby directed to surrender under orders from General Wainwright. Repeat. You are hereby directed to surrender. Details will come later."

"Thanks," I said to the colonel. "Thank you very much, sir."

I knew I had only until the details arrived to break clear. I dug up Pierson and the air corps boys out of the army barracks where they were sleeping and gave them a long list of things we'd want to reach Australia. I told them to move fast, Mindanao had shot all its ammunition into the Japs and had fallen and we were next. I told them to get all this stuff and if they found anything else to bring that along too.

Then I went looking for charts. I got on board one of the island vessels and made for the bridge. A Filipino jogged along at my elbow. "We are sinking before the Japs, sir," he said, "isn't that right, sir?"

"I guess so," I told him over my shoulder, "I guess that's right, temporarily."

"And the rats are deserting us, sir. Isn't that right, sir?"

"You can look at it that way if you want, but I don't."

"You don't, sir, because you are deserting us, too, sir, leaving us to die alone."

The only charts on board were of the Philippine Islands. There was a geography book there that had a map of the whole Pacific on one page, and the captain tore it out and gave it to me. The angry Filipino stood silently while I looked at the map. About all you could tell from it was that there was water all the way down to Australia, but hell, I thought, that's enough. If we don't have a collision with an island, we'll get to Australia all right.

"You don't have to sink before the Japs," I said to the angry Filipino, "you can come with me to Australia if you know how to pilot a banca."

"I do not desert my country, sir," he said. "I am not a rat, sir, like the Americans."

The captain looked very distressed. He had been nice to me and cordial and pained that he did not have the charts I needed and did not know where they could be got any more. Now he looked distressed, but he did not say anything.

"I think you are." I folded the chart and the map and put them in my pocket. "Yes," I said, "I think you are a rat."

Then I thanked the captain. "We will have victory yet," he assured me.

"Oh, I know that. I am certain of that. I don't even think of it because I know it so well."

The angry Filipino followed me down from the bridge.

"I do not jump off the sinking ship, sir. That is not for me. That is for the Americans."

"What is for you is to be a rat and to live off Japanese money."

He shouted over the rail after the baroto as I paddled away: "I do not desert like the Americans."

Then I went back to Colonel Cornell's headquarters to say good-by, and that's how I met Curly again.

41

7

Curly was at the headquarters with her aunt. Lt. Charlie Slain, who was a friend of the family, had brought them over for a visit. The colonel was busy, and I spoke to the aunt. Curly acted as interpreter.

The aunt had been married to a colonel in the Spanish Army. He had been loyal to the government and had been killed fighting Franco and the fascists. She was interested in PT boats, and I told her about our last engagement with the cruiser. It turned out that some friends of hers from Santander, very near the engagement, had seen it and told her about it. They had thought it was airplanes.

"Just to think," she said, "it was like a furnace blowing up with all the hot coals shooting out, and there you were in the middle of it."

"I didn't blow up."

"This whole thing of war, it looks so furious and at the same time so sad."

The destroyer had cruised around all night with lights flashing. Then the next morning there was no cruiser, just the destroyer. The destroyer had picked up a convoy of Jap ships and had gone along with them.

"You must not go to Australia," the aunt said. "It is too dangerous to try. You must not look into the face of death too long, else it will take you."

Curly translated this. Then she added, "I agree. You will only lose your life."

"Come with us to Malitbog. We have plenty of place there to hide you."

Curly translated this, too. Then she added, "You will

42

be safe there until the Americans return. I think you should do this unless you are one of those who do not want to live."

"Hell," I said. Then I said, "Excuse me, it slipped out," and said, "I want to live just as much as anybody else, but it's a question of my honor. I don't know what honor is, but I feel it in me and I have to do what honor says."

That is a fact. I wasn't handing her a line. I never thought about honor before the war, and now that I've thought of it for many years I still don't know what it is. But it's strong as steel. It just doesn't bend in you. I don't know whether I'll ever be able to figure it out, but every once in a while you get the idea it wouldn't be right to do a certain thing, and then you don't do it—or, if you do it, you're uncomfortable until you undo it.

"Anyway," I told her, "in six months I will come to Malitbog and bring you Tojo for a rickshaw boy."

"We won't have him," Curly said quickly.

Then she translated for her aunt. Her aunt seemed indignant. I heard Curly say something with "Americano" in it. "What did you say to her?" I asked.

"I said it was an American way of saying brave poetry. But my aunt says she will not let Tojo near her. She will not dirty her eyes with the sight of him."

I looked at the old lady. It did not seem to me she had spoken in the Spanish way of saying brave poetry. She seemed to me really to have meant it.

They all came down to the beach to see us off. Colonel Cornell came and Charlie Slain, Joe Price and Lt. Bill Greene and a fellow named Bullock, a wonderful fellow who had a girl with him, a mestiza, and his accordion. Bullock always brought his accordion along and played it all the time. But he played very well so it wasn't as bad as it sounds.

Later, after the surrender, Bullock tried to duck out on it. He thought this mestiza would help him, and he headed for her place. The Japs picked him up on the way to it, right near by. He had a plausible story. He said he had been cut off and was just wandering around looking for somebody to surrender to. They believed him and put him in the prison nearest to where they had picked him up.

It was near the girl's house, and Bullock smuggled a letter out to her. The letter said for her not to worry about him, he was going to escape. I suppose he had the idea he'd need clothes or something right after he got out. The girl was scared to death she would be implicated. She was a rabbit all right. She was a twitchy little rabbit of a two-bit slut. She turned the letter over to the prison commander.

The Japs played it cagy. They didn't do anything right away. Then that same night, there was a power failure in the prison. All the lights went out, and a guard rushed in and put his gun to Bullock's head and held it there until the lights went on again. There was a trial or hearing or something the same night. The letter was produced. They said the power failure was Bullock's attempt to escape. It wasn't, actually. They just said it was.

Then the next morning they asked Bullock what his last request was. He asked for his accordion. They got all the prisoners out into the yard and stood them around the block. Then Bullock walked out. He sang "God Bless America" and accompanied himself on his accordion. It was the patriotism that people had in those days. It rose up in you and made you do crazy, wonderful things. He didn't pick "The Star-Spangled Banner" because Irving Berlin's words are simpler and more direct, and it doesn't have a high part in it that your voice cracks on. Bullock didn't want his voice to crack.

The Japs asked him if he wanted a blindfold. He put a smile on his face and said no. He fastened the smile there and would not let it fade out. When they told him to get down on his knees before the block, he refused. He would not bend his knee before anything Japanese. He just stooped over to lay his neck on the block, and fellows who were there tell me that when Bullock's head fell on the earth there was still a smile on it.

Well, we had cars to go to the beach. Curly came along and her aunt and Teting, who was Loling's husband and a brand-new father at the time, and Julia Peters. Julia set herself up in the guerrilla business later as General Joan of Arc, or General Joan, or General Arc. The Filipinos were all confused and never did get it back to me straight, just as they were confused by Julia's husband, who set himself up in the guerrilla business as "General X" and stayed in it until he accumulated a pants-load of buckshot. Then he went out of business.

I went in Curly's big Buick, which she drove. Her family had a lot of money. We all whisked down to the beach in style like for a pleasure cruise.

Then I told Greene, "Bill, you're my cribbage partner and a good man, so you name our banca."

"How about *Leyte Luck*?"

I thought that was so wonderful, I shook his hand up and down. Then Charlie Slain said, "We're going to launch her for her maiden voyage. Thirteen hundred miles. Damn, boy, that's some virgin."

He had no champagne to break over the bow, but he had brought a bottle of Dewar's White Label scotch whisky.

"If you think I'm going to waste anything like this on a bow," I told him, "you're crazy."

He agreed after a while. "We'll launch her with a kiss," he said. "The belle of Tacloban will break a kiss over the skipper's bow and he'll float on it just rosy as pie to Australia."

Everything was so cheerful, it was hard to think all these fellows were sitting around waiting for Jap prison. There were hundreds of Filipinos gathered around, attracted by the preparations to sail. It was hard to think of their emotions and of how crazy was the thing we were trying to do—sail a thousand, three hundred miles of ocean without a man on board who knew a breeze-splitter from a hole in the wind.

I went on board to check the stowage. It wasn't very good. I knew about that. We had been able to get only a scattering of the things I had put down on the list. We had a sack of dried fish and some vegetables, one avocado, a little pig about two feet long, two thousand, two hundred cigars, three cases of pineapple in cans, two bottles of homemade brandy, a bunch of matches in a Mason jar, a primus stove and fifteen gallons of kerosene, some lumber, a Pioneer Compass off a P-35 that had cracked up off Ormoc, the twenty-five pint cans of milk, a pair of scissors—I'm telling these things as they come to mind—a nickel's worth of barometer, a lot of coconuts, sun helmets, a bunch of old *Reader's Digests*, about five hundred fathoms of fine rope, and some odds and ends of things like a hammer and nails and paint and for medicines a handful of salves, ointments, and cotton daubs, none of them worth anything, forty-five gallons of fresh water in five-gallon cans, ten shelter-halves, twelve lifebelts, cork, the worst, rotten kind. I worried about those lifebelts until I found out how buoyant coconuts are. If you put two under your back and two under your head, you can sleep in the water.

The crew—gosh, we sure were something out of a shanty. We could handle water if it came out of a faucet and the faucet worked. Well, let's see, there were twelve of us. Aldous McCagley was the cook, and then there was Pierson and me. Pierson was from Indiana. There were the air corps boys—Jack Crouch from Oklahoma; Oscar Smith, an ordnance man from Texas; a boy who was from Idaho, I think; Robert Snyder, a radio corps weatherman from Georgia. He promised to bring us good weather. And Joseph St. John, air corps mechanic from Philadelphia; a boy named Millikan from Pennsylvania and another fellow from Texas whose name I don't recall and still another boy. I don't remember even what he looked like, just that he was on board.

I told the boys we'd shift the stowage and get things shipshape after we got under way. Then I jumped back on the dock to say good-by.

"Don't go," Curly said to me, "please don't go. It's too dangerous." She stood with her mouth open and face all wrinkled up with worry, and she held her little fists out and shook them up and down with worry.

"Well, thanks," I said awkwardly, "thanks that you're so interested."

I got a good luck from Colonel Cornell and the others, and Bill Greene said how about a watch. I clapped my hand to my head. I had forgotten all about one, and I had a sinking feeling then wondering what vital thing else I had forgotten. Bill gave me his fine Waltham. I protested, but he said the Japs would get it anyway. Then he gave me a letter to his wife.

After that, I started to go back on board, but Charlie Slain hollered, "Hey, how about the launching," so I went over to Curly and I must have had my eyes down because I don't remember how she looked, whether she was frightened or smiling or tense or timid or annoyed or what. I thought I'd give her a little peck and break away, and started to do this and she started to give me a little peck, too, but her arms suddenly went all the way around my neck with great strength and, boy, she really hung one on.

Gee, it felt good. She was the first girl I had kissed for six or eight months, since 'way before Bataan. Then she was so pretty and nice. I grabbed ahold and I forgot what I was doing or where I was or what the whole thing was all about. There were three, four hundred people around, as well as our friends. Everybody remained quiet. Finally I could hear feet begin to shuffle and throats begin to clear. So I let Curly come up for air and broke away and jumped onto the *Leyte Luck*.

"Hoist the jib," I roared, tough as crackers.

The crew just looked at me, all except Pierson, who went over to the jib. I thought they were trying to give me the business on account of the kiss. I forgot Pierson was the only man on board who knew what a jib was.

"Get on the jib," I roared. "Take the lead out and get cracking. Two men on the poles. Lay up to the poles on the double. Hoist the mainsail."

I stomped out those orders tougher and tougher, biting them into the hide of them, until I happened to wipe my mouth with the back of my hand and found lipstick all over it. Holy cow! There I was, trying to be Captain Bligh with a baby bow of Curly's lipstick all over me.

8

We poled away from the dock. There was a stiff little breeze blowing. It looked nice and pushy to me. I didn't know any better than to say hoist the mainsail. They got the mainsail about halfway up and we took off like a shot. I had all I could do to hold on to the tiller. The crowd on the beach let out a big cheer.

We shot helter-skelter across the water and plowed crunching right into a bamboo fish trap. The crowd let out another big cheer.

"Goddamn," Pierson said to me low, "I'd give three months' pay if I didn't have to show up the United States navy's ignorance this way in front of those air corps boys."

Finally we squared away. The wind got into the mainsail again. That wind had a mind all its own. I never knew a wind could be so stubborn. It made us take out the whole fish trap and then shot us straight back towards the dock. "Hooray! Hooray!" The people were cheering again as we came towards them at flank speed. It was a hell of a way to start for Australia.

By a super effort I was able to keep us from cracking up on the dock. I pushed the tiller all the way over with every last ounce of my 160 pounds, and we just zipped along the dock, the outrigger all the way out of the water and skimming over the top of the dock, our audience trampling themselves to get back away from there.

"The outrigger!" I screamed. "Man the outriggers!" The crew was just holding on the best they could and hoping things would turn out all right. But we were heeling over into the water. "Lay up to the outriggers. Get on the Goddamn outriggers." The idea of the outriggers is to compensate for the force against the sail. You put a man or two or three on the outriggers to go as far out on them as is needed to balance the weight of the wind and keep the banca on an even keel. But my crew didn't know what an outrigger was. I couldn't point. I needed my two hands on the tiller. Finally I said, "Climb out on those things sticking out there over the water." It wasn't the kind of order that I wanted Admiral Nimitz in Honolulu to hear.

Finally the *Leyte Luck* went level. We were by then in imminent danger of running in to the opposite shore. I could see Curly's Buick driving down to the point to rescue us. I was mad. I sure was blister mad. We were within fifteen yards of the shoal water and I could look down and see the coral and the tropical fish swimming around.

Then the wind must have changed because I was able to steer away and into the channel. I went without looking back at the people on the shore or Curly or anybody. But in the channel we started shipping spray. The pig didn't like it. He waltzed around squealing a little bit. He was lashed fairly secured. His ears had been pierced and a rope run through the holes, but finally he broke off his ear tips and jumped overboard.

He was our only fresh meat, but I didn't know how to stop the boat or slow it or turn it around. The pig kept swimming after us, but he fell farther and farther astern and I just had to let him keep on swimming until he couldn't swim any more.

"You see how it is," I told my crew. "So don't any of you guys fall overboard."

9

It took me two days and two nights of fooling around to discover the trick of turning the wind into a motor for the *Leyte Luck*.

There were two strikes on us anyway from the southwest monsoon that prevails in those waters in the summer months and that we had to tack into. The third strike was the fact that we had only one mast and such a big sail on it. If we had had two masts, I could just have luffed the forward sail and held down the aft one. Then the wind would have brought her right around. But with one mast, I finally figured out the best way was to get up speed on one tack, then let go the stay rope and give her hard right rudder. Then, traveling on that momentum, we released the mainsail. Three or four men pushed the boom clear on over. That made her lose her forward momentum and start backing down, and I reversed the rudder and the stern swung right on around. I don't think there is another sailboat in the world that would have to be handled like that.

The crew took the experimenting pretty well. Once in a while one of them would get mad and I'd say, "Christ, I'm doing the best I can." I was getting enough guff from the *Leyte Luck* without getting more from them. But those were good boys. I've found that most of our boys are good people. We were all doing a crazy thing, but we were in it together. Then when something I tried actually worked, I'd say, "This is it, boys. Now we're going places." Then we'd fall flat on our face in some way. When I felt something was right, I insisted on it. I was skipper and we'd do it even if it was wrong. It looked to us then like the banca or the Japs. The boys preferred the banca, all except one—this fellow from Idaho. He got seasick even before we hit the channel, and when we pulled into the beach on a small island to renew some mainsail ropes that were getting chafed, why, he decided he had had enough and lit out. I never heard of him again and don't know what happened to him. He just took two lifebelts and went.

The nights were calm and there was usually a light breeze. I set a heel-and-toe watch for Pierson and myself, four on and four off. I let the rest sleep through the night, cramped side by side and head to foot on the flooring of the deck. Generally there was no moon until early in the morning. Then it would come up pale as lemon. But at night the dark coast would slide by, and the black water. I would watch the phosphorescent little organisms in the water to see if we were making any speed. As the boat went by, they got excited and turned on a little light. The side of the banca would slide with a small hiss past the angry, motionless, frightened little lights.

Then we hit a place where the sea bottom was shallow and unequal. It made for a remarkable tide. The water across the whole center there was as flat and solid-looking as plate glass and outside the smooth parts there would be agitated little ruffles, huge washboards full of them. What was happening was that the tide would hit this unequal bottom and climb straight up it and through to the top of the water. We got sucked into the current there and went through boiling, with no sail or anything. We'd go spanking along a little way, then hit a whirlpool and go around and around and around for fifteen minutes, with no more control than over a balloon in mid-air, then shoot out of it and into the current and whiz along until another whirlpool grabbed us and twirled us around and around for another fifteen minutes.

Another time a squall dumped a heavy rain and high wind on us. It was sheltered water there, fortunately. We kept the sail up because we didn't know how to get it down fast enough. We had a four-way block system, and we had to have a man jiggle the sail down when we wanted to furl it. Well, this wind put its big hairy head right into the sail and just kept it there butting.

The only time I've ever gone faster over water in my life is on a PT boat. The banca was a marvelous sailing vessel because it was so narrow.. It knifed through the water. It took four of us on the tiller. The rest just sat there with their mouths open like they had been hit in the stomach. It was as if we were plowing. The bow turned up mountain-sized furrows of creaming water on either side. I looked astern once, and believe me, anybody who was there will tell you, there was a wake full of thin white bubbles for two hundred yards. I never heard of anything like that before or since, but that was the way it was this time.

It lasted for about ten minutes. When it was over, I said, "Boys, I'll tell you, I'm not accustomed to this kind of thing. Let's break open one bottle."

Snyder had never taken a drop in his life. But he held out his hand for the bottle and said, "Give it to me, boy."

On the morning of May 18, about six o'clock, just dawn, the watch woke me up and said he saw something funny walking towards us and would I take a look at it. It was what the natives call a *Chibasco,* a solid wall of rain about a mile wide with very high winds in it. It seemed to be standing on the water and walking across it slowly, but it came like a cyclone.

If I had known then what I know now, we would have been all right. The first law of the navy is never to belay a shcet, but there was ours, secure in a seagoing lash. If the sheet had been free, then the *Chibasco* would just have blown the sail out of its way and nothing more would have happened. With the sheet belayed like that, the sail couldn't get out of the way and she turned the boat over. There was a kind of whoosh like a slow buffeting snort. Then the boat was over on her side before I even seemed to feel the wind hitting us.

I took one look at the *Chibasco* drumming towards us. "Come into the wind!" I yelled. But the fellow on the tiller—I forget just who it was at the time—couldn't. It was too late. There was already a solid muscle of water against him. Gray-black fists of air fell on me. "Outrigger!" I screamed at the top of my lungs, then ran out on the outrigger myself. The outrigger went straight up into the air like a telegraph pole. I clung to the end of it. The fists of air were already beginning to frazzle out. Then the air became cottony and I looked down through it and saw the side of the boat lifted up towards me. I slid down the outrigger and landed on the side of the boat without getting my feet wet.

10

There weren't any injuries. All the sleeping people just got rolled into the sea and woke up swimming. The *Chibasco* passed before their minds were all the way out of the cobwebs of sleep. The light of the rising sun grew over the sky, and the sea became calm and lifted and fell slow and calm even while they were still splashing around in it. They didn't know what had happened. They hollered to me to ask was it a whale or a submarine, or what had we hit that had dumped us.

The sail floated out flat before us. I thought its surface tension might be keeping the banca from uprighting itself, so we worked to furl it. But, contrary to expectations, when we got the sail taken all the way in, the *Leyte Luck* turned her bottom to the sky. Then that was that. Yes, that was good-by to her.

We had come about two hundred miles in our cruise. We were just about eight miles offshore at the time. We could make out a lighthouse on the point there—Cawit Point on Mindanao Island. I told the fellows I was going to swim for it to get help.

"I'm not going to tell any of you to do it who don't want to," I pointed out. "But a Jap boat might come along and try to rescue us."

It looked like a long swim to me. I was not sure I could make it. I knew the more there were who tried, the more chance there was of someone getting through.

First two said to count them in, then one more and another and another until finally there were seven. Earl Homan dove under the boat and came up with breakfast for us. He made three trips. He brought up a quart jar half full of fresh water, two cans of milk, a canteen cup and two jars of jam—peach and raspberry jam, or something that tasted like raspberry jam. We opened the cans of milk with the canteen cup, banging a hole with the handle. I poured the milk into the water. It was a very weak solution, but it was the only way to have enough to go around. Then we ate the jam with our fingers. We couldn't eat much. It was too sweet. When you've got only sweet stuff, you just can't get down much of it.

I had fifteen dry cigarettes left. Nobody had any matches that would work, but I happened to have a pencil flashlight in my pocket and I took off the lens and focused the sun's rays on the cigarette end. We had one each. I gave the leftovers to the fellows who were not going to try to swim it. Three of them didn't know how to swim and the other fellow—the one whose name and face I can't seem to be able to remember at all—just didn't want to.

While we were sitting on the boat smoking, McCagley said he thought the mast was dragging on the bottom.

"We are now in the Mindanao Deep," I told him.

"It can't be very deep. I hear it scraping on the bottom."

I had to laugh. The Mindanao Deep has the deepest water in the world. It's thirty-five thousand feet there to the bottom.

"Gee," he cried, "are you going to swim in all that much over your head?"

"We are intending to use only the top part of it," I told him.

There was not a boat anywhere or a cloud or a bird or a sign of human life or fish life or a splash or anything, just the sea lifting and falling slow and calm like the sides of a sleeping animal and the overturned boat lifting and falling like a fly on it. We were the fleas on the fly.

"Well," I said, "everybody defecate."

We lined up and did it over the side. Everybody did it. They knew the importance of it.

They wanted to know about sharks.

"Sharks won't hurt you," I said. "That's a superstition."

"Suppose they're superstitious?"

"Oh hell, sharks bite you only if you're dead."

I didn't know what I was talking about at the time, but I was skipper and was supposed to have the answers. I told them if they got into a current not to fight it and if the tide took them not to fight it, but just to go along swimming steadily.

"Don't stop to rest," I said. "Don't stop moving yourself because your muscles will bunch up and you will need a monkey wrench to unscrew yourself.

"Okay," I cried at last, "what are we waiting for, the *Normandie?*"

"Come on and give 'em hell," shouted Millikan and jumped in crabwise, flailing his arms and laughing and making a big splash.

"Let's get on the ball there." I clapped my hands together. "Let's give it the old college try."

Then the seven of us were in the water. There was some shouting around at first, fellows calling back to those who had stayed behind, "Come on in, the water's fine," and saying, "Look, look, I got a mermaid."

"Pipe down!" I shouted. "Anybody who wastes breath talking," I shouted, "is giving himself that much less chance to live."

The fellows settled down after that. They settled down abruptly. The feeling of how abruptly they settled down took hold of me, too, and then I became afraid, too.

Homan was a beautiful swimmer. He was the best there and one of the best I have ever seen. He took off all his clothes at the start. All he wore was a little play shirt. I slid into the water with all my clothes on, including some black tennis shoes that I had gotten in Tacloban. I was afraid of coral cutting my feet when we got to shore. Then I wanted to get across the beach fast and into the trees in case there were Japs watching. I took a lifebelt, too. I took the worst one to give the other fellows the better ones because I was the only officer. The straps were torn so I just put it loose under me as a pontoon.

I swam alongside Pierson. We were both navy. Then I thought he might need a little moral support. I noticed he was carrying a two-pound tin of Hills Bros. coffee inside his lifejacket. It was a vacuum tin and buoyant, but it lumped out the lifejacket.

"That's a stewhead thing to do," I told him.

"No," he said, "we're going to need coffee bad when we get through with this."

I didn't want to spend energy arguing. I thought he'd rid himself of it soon enough. I swam the Australian crawl. If I had to do it over again I'd choose another stroke to keep my head and eyes and nose out of the water as much as possible. But the crawl came easiest to me and anyway once I started I didn't dare change. After a couple hours, every time I slacked stroke I could feel my muscles begin to knot in me and I thought if I ever stopped I'd never get them unknotted.

Pierson and I swam thirteen hours like mackerels, without stopping moving once. After four for five hours, I let the lifejacket slide out from under me. It had rubbed my chest raw. Then I kicked off my shoes. They seemed to be holding me back. I saw a sailboat and I tried to shout to it, but I couldn't make myself heard very far. I tried splashing. Pierson splashed with me. But it was 'way in back of us. It fooled around there, picking up some of the slower swimmers. I found out later those fellows tried to make the boatmen understand about us and about the Leyte Luck, but they could hardly talk any more they were so tired and after a few minutes they gave up trying to flap around in sign language and just pooped out.

Then there were locusts, like our grasshoppers. Out in the Philippines, there are millions of them. A mass of them will get into a high wind and just blow along with it like a cloud. If the wind stops over the ocean, they fly around until they are tired. Then they light on the water and die. Pierson and I swam into a square mile of them. First there were millions of dead ones just floating. Our arms hit them. Then we came to those still living. They'd light on anything until the water splashed them off. They lit on the back of my head, scores of them, brawling silently for space, standing silently on each other. I dipped my head under the water and they'd whir off. Then they'd come back again, whirring and piling on, jostling each other, and nudging and standing on each other and pushing each other off into the water. It was like a battlefield there, only so quiet. They were all dying so quietly. It took about half an hour to work through them.

After swimming seven hours, we were farther from the beach than when we had started. The tide was carrying us on a tangent out to sea. I knew if we just kept going, the tide would change and help us.

"Mr. Richardson," called Pierson, "I don't think I can make it alone."

It took me a long time to make up my mind to answer him. If he couldn't make it alone, then I wasn't going to make it either. As a matter of fact, at the time I thought I couldn't make it alone myself. I thought I would just have to stop working. Then my muscles would knot and I would never be able to unknot them. I would just lie there knotted up. As I remember, I didn't think of what would happen after that. I just thought of myself lying like a hopeless snarl of rope in the water.

"Mr. Richardson, please help me," called Pierson.

I lifted my head out of the water then. I didn't stop moving my arms and legs, so they were all right. But I could feel the muscles of my neck bunch up until it felt like oyster shells there.

"Can't you see the trees are getting bigger?" I shouted.

"I can't see anything. I can't hold my eyes open any more."

"Take a look at the trees. They're a hell of a lot clearer to see now."

I begrudged the energy I used shouting, but I begrudged more spending the energy to swim closer to him. I put my head back into the water. The muscles of my neck grated and ground like oyster shells that you step on. I swam on a little more. Then I lifted my head again. The pain of that was like it had cut my heart open. Pierson was looking at the trees and swimming.

"I can't see the trees," he said.

"They're clear as hell." I couldn't see them either. "I can count leaves."

"My eyes are just bags of salt."

"Don't swim with your eyes."

We had six more hours of swimming to go.

Things got better for us after that. I think we got dehydrated or something. I think, as the water worked out of us, we were lighter and swam faster and easier. The sun went down. The darkness seemed to come up out of the sea. I know the common expression is that night falls. But actually I'd say the night rises. There was not a shadow there on that sea, but I remember when I swung my hand over my head it flashed white. The water dripping off it looked all rosy golden. Then as my hand came down to the sea it darkened darker and darker and then black. I had never thought of the night rising up to the sky before, but I saw it then for the first time and have noticed it all the time since. After minutes, my hand coming over my head was gray, then black, and the drops of water dripping off it became gray and then had the black oil-like look of night water while the day was still in the sky up above. The night rose higher and higher and finally covered the sky, and the longer we swam the better we swam. I am not sure of the scientific reason, but it was so. At the end we seemed to have as much energy as when we had started and we could put on a burst of speed and fight the current in order not to be swept clear of the point.

Finally I could touch bottom. Pierson stood a little behind me. He was taller. We stood in water to our chins. Our legs and our whole bodies were trembling. The trembles went up and down me like schools of shivering little fish darting. There was a whole splash and twirl to each tremble. I stood looking at Pierson and he stood looking at me. We didn't move too much for a long time.

"I've still got the coffee," he said.

I remember I wanted to say something in answer, but I was too tired to think of words.

Then we took a few steps towards the beach. It couldn't have been more than a few steps because when we stopped the water reached to our necks.

"What if there are Japs?" asked Pierson.

"There are none."

"Maybe in the lighthouse there."

"The lighthouse is all dark."

"Oh yes," Pierson said. "I was too tired to think of that."

The water held us up. It seemed to reach under our

arms and hold us like with hands and seemed to be a body holding our backs so we didn't topple over.

"How are we going to walk all that way to the beach?" I asked Pierson. It looked to be about eighty or a hundred feet.

"I'd like to lie down," he said. "I'd like to lie down with my face down in a mattress."

The thing is, it was a mistake to have stopped swimming. We had been going along all right, until we stopped. We should have swum right up to the beach and then pulled ourselves out of the water and just lain down there. But it was too late now to do anything about that.

"We'd better start," I said. "Maybe the tide is coming in and then we'll have twice as far to walk."

But he didn't start. I knew if I started, he'd start. I was the officer. But I couldn't start. I thought if I began to walk I'd fall down and drown. I didn't feel I could swim any more. But I couldn't walk either. I just couldn't budge my muscles to walk.

"What are we going to do," asked Pierson, "when the water gets below our knees and doesn't hold us up any more?"

"We're going to fall down."

"And then what are we going to do?"

"We can crawl then on our hands and knees."

"The coral will chop us into hamburger."

"We can float and pull ourselves along with our fingers."

"That's a good idea. Well, let's go."

But I couldn't start, and he couldn't.

"Hell," he said, "we can drown here just as well as in the middle of the ocean. We'd better start walking."

"Yes." I tried to take a step but I couldn't. "You can drown in a bathtub. All you need for drowning is to cover your mouth and nose." I tried again to take a step and again couldn't.

"You know," Pierson said, "I can't walk an inch to save my life."

"I can't either." I felt like laughing, but I was too tired to let the laugh out of me.

So we just stayed there. We didn't talk any more. We

just stood still and let the water hold us up and felt all the time we were falling down in it.

Then a light began to bounce on the water. I thought it was some kind of strange animal at first. I looked at it quite a few minutes wondering what it was. Then I realized it was a baroto. Homan had made the beach in eight hours and had sent two of them to look for the rest of us. But they had been afraid in the night and had just hugged the shore.

"Oi!" I called in the Philippine way, "oi there! Oi! Over here."

They dragged us over the side and I went to sleep while they still had their hands on me dragging.

11

The next thing I saw we were in a nipa hut and there was a man lying there who seemed familiar to me, yet I could not quite place him. It took me a long time to realize it was Homan. He was so sunburned and he looked so old. He had swum with only his play shirt on. He was sunburned all over because he had swum all the strokes there are, including backstroke, but the part of him that was worst was his behind. It had never been touched by the sun's rays before, I guess. There was regular baby skin there, I guess, but now it looked all swollen up and really mutilated. He couldn't bear to put anything on it, even a kimono they had given him. When he had landed on the beach and fallen there, there had been some women washing themselves or something and they had all run screaming away. That was the last he remembered before passing out, their running screaming away. He woke up being carried along by them with palm leaf over him. They had brought him to the home of a schoolteacher, where Pierson and I had been brought, too.

I wanted water and I wanted to go back to sleep. They shook their heads no when I asked for water. I thought they meant no understand and tried sign language. I tried to show myself swallowing and to say "Glug glug" but it hurt too much and I felt feverish tired, so I thought the hell with it and went to sleep. They made me very warm. They took off all my clothes and laid me on a dry bed and put sheets over me—the Filipinos don't have blankets—and laid all their clothes over the sheets.

Then, two hours later, about midnight I guess, they woke me up. They took my shoulder and shook it until I stopped fighting them off and woke up. When my mind became clear I thought for a minute it was Japs and really sprang up, but it was just to give me a little warm clear soup. There was just enough there to wet the bottom of the cup. It made one dainty, ladylike swallow. But I couldn't swallow it. My throat just constricted tight as a clam. Salt water had inflamed it too much.

"Drink," the schoolteacher's wife commanded. "Swallow."

I squeezed a few drops down. Tears of pain came into my eyes. I shook my head and took up the cup to spit the soup out.

She snatched the cup out of my hand. "You must swallow," she said, "or you will not get well."

I shook my head no and she shook her head yes. Then I put my head all the way back. I closed my eyes to hide the tears that I knew would come. Then I let the soup go down in a gulp. It was like running a hot soldering iron down my throat.

But I fell asleep with the tears still wet in my eyes.

They woke us up every two hours all night and gave us about an ounce of soup each. I took it lying down after the first time. I put it in the side of my mouth and let it slide down in little bits, sort of. There was a feeling in my throat after each swallow like a steamshovel claw closing. Then, in the morning, they fed us part of the pulp of a camote, a sort of sweet potato. Those people knew just what to do. We had been brought to a little fishing village, a barrio of about one hundred population, and there doesn't seem to be anything the sea can think up to do to a man that a fishing village hasn't had some experience with.

"Mr. Richardson, sir," said Pierson when he woke up in the morning, "is that you?"

"Why?" I said. "Is there something the matter with me?" I thought maybe his eyes had gone bad on him.

"You look like a scarecrow."

"Well, boy," I said, "I can't see any crow falling in love with you either."

Then Jack Crouch was brought in. He had hallucinations. He kept seeing ships sailing by him without stopping. "Oi!" he kept yelling, "help, oi!" But none of the ships in his hallucinations ever stopped, and he'd groan and fall silent until suddenly he was yelling to another ship. He had been in the water twenty-four hours.

After that Millikan came in. He had been in the water twenty-five hours. He walked in. They were holding on to him, but not carrying him. He walked in slow and bent over and he had that look on his face that you get when you think you are going to die.

All eleven of us had been taken in one way or another from the sea. Five of us had swum our way out. Two had been picked up by the sailboat I had vainly called to, and the remaining four had been taken off the bottom of the *Leyte Luck* the next morning by a boat from the village.

I asked the schoolteacher about the Japs.

"Oh, they are far away," he said, "eight kilometers."

That did not seem very far to me.

"They don't return. They came once. They searched the houses. Then they made a speech and then they went away."

"What kind of a speech?"

"That we are brothers."

"Are you?"

"There is no one in this village who is a brother to the Japs or cousin or friend or likes them."

"It is dangerous to hide Americans," I said. "I must know the truth how the people feel."

"The truth is as I said. The Japs came with guns, and we were quiet to make them go away. They searched with guns. When they made their speech, they held their guns. You came without guns and are safe. They would not be safe without guns."

"Is it known that the Japs will kill those who hide Americans?"

"The Americans are our brothers."

"But is it known?"

"It was said on May 20 by the Japs that all Americans and our soldiers who have not yet surrendered are now outlaws and bandits. But Japs' saying does not make it so."

"They talk with guns."

"Yes, but we listen with our hearts."

It was arranged that we should scatter among the people of the village so as not to put too great a strain on the food supply of any one family, and it was arranged, too, that if the Japs should approach warning would be given us and we would take off for the jungle.

Millikan was the only one of us who did not recover. He had had malaria before, and now it recurred in him. He shook terribly, and his teeth knocked together with the chills so loud I was afraid they would break. Then he got dysentery. After that, a foul yellow bile kept coming out of his mouth. For hours, then, it was hard to tell whether he was still alive. I would listen to his heart. It made a strange sound. You could almost hear a wheeze in it and a bubbling. We got a doctor for him, but by the morning of June 3 he was dead.

I knew of a Dutch priest in a near-by barrio. I walked to him and asked if he would perform the burial. He said he couldn't, the Japanese might construe it as rebellion. "You must turn the body over to them, I will accompany it," he said. "You need not appear. It will be to them a lone body that has been found. When the body has been turned over to them. I will see that it is buried properly."

"Render unto Caesar," he said.

"You will pardon me, father," I could not hold myself back. "My own father was of the cloth. I have been brought up in religion. But when it comes to rendering unto Caesar, there are some men who should be rendered first into their own fat."

"My boy, my boy, I forgive you your anger, but I have the population to think of as well as my own conscience."

The population gave me a white duck suit to bury Millikan in and a coffin and an American flag and a brass band like the one in that little island we had stopped at, full of oompah, to follow the body to the cemetery and a fine plot in the cemetery with a good view of the sea and a wooden headstone like the best there was there.

I dressed Millikan myself and did the most I could to make him look nice before nailing down the coffin. I wanted to shave him, but there was no razor. Then the band oompahed us out to the cemetery and the whole population followed and grouped themselves around the open grave.

The priest was there, too. I thought for a moment he had changed his mind, but he said no, he had just come with the others.

"Then, father," I asked him, "will you please leave?"

"My boy, my dear boy."

"We do not want you here, father. We want the burial to be in the sight of God."

We had four American rifles there that had been retrieved from the *Leyte Luck*. The boys lined up on opposite sides of the grave. The teacher stood beside me to interpret for the population, only about a third of whom knew English. It seemed up to me to make the funeral talk. Everybody looked to me to do it and I did the best I could.

I remember I said, "This is one of our boys," something to that effect, and then, "He didn't ask to come over here, and maybe he didn't die fighting bullets. But he died doing what he thought was right. He died trying to keep himself in the war against the Japanese rather than surrender to them. There will be a happy day again soon for all of us, and then his remains can go back to America. He leaves a daughter of three or four. She can be proud of him the rest of her life. His wife can be proud of him. It's an accomplishment in life for a man to do something to make his wife and child proud of him. His parents can be proud they raised a son who was no quitter."

"There is not the word for quitter in our dialect," the schoolteacher said.

"A man is not a quitter who, once he makes a fight his own, can be stopped only by death."

"Oh yes, we have the word for that in Visayan."

"He did not live a long time," I said, "not as long as most expect to, but at least people who knew him will remember him. And his memory will be a good father to his daughter. For the rest of the history of America and of your country, all his family that comes after him will be able to say, when asked, 'He died fighting the Japs,' and it will be something to say that will describe him and give heart and pride to whoever in his family comes after him.

"All right, boys," I said after that, "you can go ahead now."

They fired three volleys. The drum out of the band rolled. None of us knew the right procedure, but we tried to remember what we had seen and make it look nice. There was a woman there who knew the Catholic ritual. She led the prayer and band and the whole population joined in the hymns. Then we covered the grave and saluted it and went away, carrying the American flag because it was the only one in the barrio and we wanted to show that no matter what happened the flag went marching on.

I thought that right after the funeral, while the lesson of it was still fresh in their minds, would be a good time to put up to the boys what we should do next.

"Okay, boys," I said, "here's the dope. Now that we are getting rested up, how about taking another crack at Australia?"

Nobody said anything. We were all out on the ground there in front of the schoolteacher's hut where I was living.

"I've saved fifty pesos out of the wreck that I had in my pocket," I said. "We'll take our time this time and do it right. We'll just get another banca and stock it up good and wait until we find a Filipino who knows his stuff to go with us. We'll make it down there all right that way."

They were silent. Some of them looked down and some looked away and nobody said anything.

"Well, talk up," I said. "Let's bat the thing around. If we don't get out of here, I think we'll just have to surrender."

"I don't see why." I forget who said that, but one of them did.

"Everybody else surrendered. There's fifth columnists around and no medicine. Look what happened to Millikan."

"That's what we're looking at, that we'll have to swim again."

"No, it wasn't the swimming. It was the no medicines.

There are more of us bound to get sick here sooner or later and there will still be no medicines. And what about that order by the Japs, that if you didn't surrender by May 20 you're an outlaw and a bandit. What the hell is that to be?"

We got nowhere fast. They couldn't see my point at all. I guess, if it comes to that, I couldn't see it too clearly myself and was just talking there because after all I was still drawing pay on the navy books as an officer. What it amounted to was that I had given them more or less of an order that they didn't intend to obey, and now I had to back down. I couldn't make it to Australia all by myself.

"Well," I said at last, "I vote for trying to make it. I can't tell you to try if you don't want to, but if there's a group gets up, just three or four, you can count me in."

But there was no group. There never did get to be one. And that was that.

12

Through almost the whole summer of 1942, the part of the Philippines where I was remained quiet. The Japs weren't there in much force, not enough force to cover everywhere because their main army had rolled on south, east, and west from there, and only dribs and drabs had been left behind. But there had been an amputation. A protecting army had been amputated from its people, and the people lay sick a long time.

My boys and myself had what amounted to a racket. We spent all together something more than six months in and around where we had foundered. The life was lazy and pleasant. I went spear fishing and swimming and wrote down as a book the record of our PT squadron's experiences. I found typewriter, paper, and carbon paper in a closed schoolhouse. (All schools had been closed by order of President Quezon to keep Japs from indoctrinating Filipino children. They really were, with few exceptions, closed even though their teachers were starving.) There was no ribbon in the typewriter, so I wrote on the carbon paper.

Every now and then we would move. Mostly so that the burden of feeding us would not be too heavy on any one family. But partly on account of the Japs. They would send out an occasional patrol.

"Oh sir, yes sir, the Americans were here, sir. I saw them with my own eyes, sir, but they left three or four months ago."

That's what the Filipinos would say when maybe we had ducked out five minutes before, pulling on our pants as we ran.

About 70 per cent of the people were afraid of the Japanese. They were nervous before us. While they did not deny us hospitality, they were just as glad if we did not stay too long. The other 30 per cent did not give a damn about the Japs. They wanted us to stay forever. But all the people, whether nervous or not, whether scared of the Japs or not . . . well, the proof of how they felt was that we wandered around freely, and wherever we were, even if in a strange barrio or just passing some farm out in the hills somewhere, when Japs would come near people would run to tell us and show us the safest way out. Some of this, of course, may have been to keep themselves out of trouble with the Japs, but nobody told the Japs anything. And it was impossible for a Jap to hide anywhere to spy on us. He simply could not get enough people to help him conceal his movements. He was in the house of his enemies. We were secure because we were in a land of friends.

This was true for most Americans, and there were Americans scattered all over the place. Some had just not surrendered and had hid out in the hills. Some had broken out of prison. Some, like ourselves and Tom Jurika and Cap and Mrs. Martin, had foundered on the way to Australia, then made shore and just holed up there.

But it didn't make you feel too good always to keep running from the enemy, pulling on your pants as you ran. And about September 1, an American by the name of Abbott and another named Tony Heratik came out in the open with how a surprising number of people seemed to feel. Abbott is originally from Arizona, where he was a cattleman. I don't know what part of the country Tony came from. As I remember, they both had been air corps boys. Abbott looks like that Zeke character in *Esquire,* tall, lanky, slow-looking, with a full, black, bushy beard. He had vowed not to shave until the Americans came back.

These boys had been hiding out near Balingasag. That was their town. They came in every time they needed something and everybody knew them there and would swap the time of day with them. September 1 they walked in as usual. There were three Japs there who had come to do some shopping—a captain and two enlisted men. In those days, the Japs wandered around everywhere just as if they had already won the war. They did it until the guerrillas taught them not to. People were quick to warn the Americans of the three Japs there. They expected the Americans to go away, but these two boys were tired of running.

"We are going to run them the hell out of town," Abbott said.

"Yes," agreed Tony, "they don't belong here."

The boys had Browning automatic rifles. The Japs were armed, too, but they were scared. They ran into the biggest church in town, a famous wooden church about a hundred years old. They ran up into the steeple and then

Browning Automatic Rifle

there was no way to get them out. Abbott and Heratik didn't have mortars or machine guns or even hand grenades. They couldn't spare the time to starve them out. So they set the church on fire. Nobody stopped them, or protested. The church was worth two or three hundred thousand pesos. It had great historical value for some reason or other that I am not clear on. But it burned right down to the ground, just like an ordinary building, and now its ruins have even greater historical value. This was the match that ignited the whole part of the island where I was.

When the fire got going good, one of the Japs jumped out of the steeple and smashed himself dead against the earth, but Abbott emptied a whole clip into him anyway to make sure. The other two let themselves be burned down with the church. Then Abbott and Heratik went on about their errands, the people saying "Good" to them, "A fine accomplishment, sir."

The bamboo telegraph carried the news of this event all over everywhere. Americans nobody ever knew had been there turned up walking the jungle paths to Balingasag. If there was a war on, they wanted in on it. They had heard the Americans had "taken" Balingasag. The Jap answer was to descend on the town with a reinforced patrol. They killed one Filipino soldier who hadn't been able to run away in time, but they didn't burn the town down or mince up the civilians with their bayonets. Not that time. They were still in the "co-prosperity" period of their program.

But the idea had caught on. "Kill Japs." It appears like a simple idea, but nobody had seemed to know how to go about it before. Now they thought they knew. Get a gun and shoot it into them. In about two weeks, there were some fifty separate guerrilla bands wandering around the island, each with a proud name and an ambitious leader.

It was no trouble at all to get these bands started. The Japs had made a lot of men jobless and homeless. The Filipino policy of non-co-operation in Jap "co-prosperity" had made more men jobless—schoolteachers, for instance, political servants of one kind or another, bus and truck drivers, small boatmen whose craft had been confiscated or wrecked, former Filipino soldiers wandering around loose. If these men were not guerrillas, they were bums. As guerrillas, they had a respectable and even advantageous position in their communities. All doors were open to them. They were national heroes.

But it is always the adventurers and desperadoes who are the first to move, and the wrong people got hold of these bands at the start. The thing was that in the Visayan

72

Islands there were hardly any politics on an ideological basis. It was almost all on a personal basis. A strong man or a passionate talker attracts a personal following and builds up a machine. Then he is a power in politics. The opposition to the Japanese was all on a nationalist basis.

There were a few desperate poor who saw the war as a chance to equalize things. In some cases there were guerrilla bands who killed off the local rich and even their children to prevent them inheriting land. In the province of Pampanga, the agricultural land was in the hands of maybe a dozen families. They ground their tenants very hard. A tenant who would live within his income and not borrow money at usurious rates from his landlord would be kicked off his lot. The landlords didn't want the children of their tenants to become educated. Naturally enough, since education is an enemy of oppression. If the landlord knew a child was attending high school, all his relatives would be kicked out. There had been many cases of kids going to high school secretly like in America they sneak off to a juke joint for hot swing. His relatives would tell the landlord he was a bum and had run away. Well, the odds against landlords like that living through the operations of these guerrilla bands are fairly high. But mostly it was just that the Filipinos had come to feel themselves a nation. They liked the Americans because the Americans had promised them independence and they were sure the promise would be made good. They didn't like the Japs because they just didn't believe a word the Japs said. There was an election before the war where a fellow in southern Luzon, near Leyte, ran for office on a pro-Japanese program. He was the only one in the history of the islands, and he was snowed under.

The Filipinos were afraid of the Japs. That's mostly what they didn't like about them. They were afraid of what the Japs would do when they got a foot in the door. They had a law preventing anybody who was not a Filipino or American from owning land. This law goes back about fifteen years. It was aimed directly at the Japs and the Jap answer to that was to bring in American-born and Hawaiian-born Japanese and form landholding corporations with them. They were just dummy corporations, and the Filipino attitude to "The Greater East Asia Co-Prosperity Sphere" that the Japs brought into the islands with their bayonets was that this was just another dummy corporation. No, the Filipinos are not fools, and they were afraid, too, the Japs would do what they had heard the Japs had done in Korea and Formosa. The story was they had forbidden Formosans to marry each other, or Koreans to marry each other. If these people wanted to get married, they had to marry Japs. In that way the Japs made sure to incorporate their conquests into their empire. The Filipinos didn't want to marry Japs. They just didn't want to, and they just didn't want them around at all.

However, where politics consist of personalities, where the political platform is to kill Japs, and where desperadoes and outcasts become thus the first to jump in, then the whole complexion there is likely to be pretty pimply. I investigated carefully. My boys and myself wanted to get in on a going war, too. A guerrilla band would descend on a barrio and identify itself as fighters for freedom. Then they would levy on the people—take clothes, food, guns, whatever they could get. Women, too. The people at first were glad to give. The women were glad to go and give their very pretty or comfortable all for their country. But as these men fattened and still no Japs were killed, the people became a little chary. Then these guerrilla bands would simply confiscate. They'd spend the afternoon searching house to house, store to store, and taking what they wanted, their guns ready to reply to a protest. They could kill anybody they felt like simply by describing him as a fifth columnist. In the evening, they would take over the town square and make fiery speeches.

"Kill the Japanese! Strike the murdering dwarfs from the land of our peaceful shores! They have come here to rob us, not to protect us!"

Long hours of speeches. Then they would go back into the hills to live off what they had confiscated. When they needed more, they'd come back. It was a racket. The bands fought each other like gangs over territory. They spent more time fighting each other than fighting Japs. One band did not want another band to muscle in on its territory because that would dry up the loot too fast and the swag would have to be split too many ways. The bands were constantly trying to move over into the fatter territories.

The Japs were not "so sorry" over it. They thought it would drive the civilian population into their arms as the bringers of law and order. They underestimated the fierceness of the Filipinos' desire for freedom. I underestimated it, too.

"This is not for us," I told my men. "Those fellows are on the wrong track. They're not going any place except someday the civilians are going to turn on all of them. We ought to keep America out of it."

I did not understand the Filipino people. They never turned against anybody who put himself in a position where he might have to fight Japs. That was enough, just putting yourself in a position where the Jap was your enemy. The people were willing to take robbery and worse, much, much worse, rather than take the Japs.

When I think of it now and think how other Americans got into the guerrilla movement, I feel that maybe I stayed out of it at first, not so much because I underestimated the Filipinos and didn't want to dirty our country's reputation by helping identify it with something that smelled rank as because I am just not the type. It takes all kinds to make war. It takes fighting men and technicians. Every man who gets shot at and shoots back likes to think of himself as a fighting man, so this is very hard for me to say. But I guess I am the technician type, and although I did not realize it at the time and am only just now, in thinking back on the whole thing, beginning to become aware of it, that must be mostly why I stayed out. There wasn't any room in those bands for the technician type, and technician types don't start their own bands. That's for fighting men.

Take a fellow like Tom Baxter. His story is a fair sample of what the guerrilla was like for the non-technician type—the fighting man type. I think Baxter's first name is Tom. We always called him "Long." He wasn't very tall, about five feet nine, but he was taller than the Filipinos and they gave him the nickname Long. I think he came from somewhere in the East. He's a boy in his early twenties and I remember he used to tell me if he ever got out alive and collected his back pay, he was going to blow it all in in a week. The week would be so big he'd have a hang-over the rest of his life. "Ten years later," he said, "just the memory of it will give me a hang-over and will spare me the expense of accumulating a new one."

Long had been an enlisted man in the air corps stationed at Del Monte. He cut loose and started hiking across the hills. The hills there are empty of all people except Manobos and Minandayans. Except that the Manobos live in lean-tos built against trees and the Minandayans live on platforms in the trees, they are six of one and half a dozen of another. Maybe they know there is a war going on, but they've got their own wars to worry about. Their tribal feuds have been going on for thousands of years.

The Minandayans were a very interesting people to me. For a house they built themselves a bamboo platform thirty to fifty feet off the ground in a crotch of a tree. They put a regular roof over it woven of grasses. They went up and down it on a knotted rope, using their hands and big toe to go up the knots as fast as we go up stairs. At night they bring all their dogs up into the "house" with them because their dogs are their livelihood. They hunt with their dogs and use them as protection against rival tribesmen. Their eating habits are not the kind an American, fresh out of even an army chow line, can thrive on overnight. They eat snakes (mostly python), wild pig, monkey, and what they find, but it's what they do with their meat that really knocks you. The meat is all tough, their teeth generally bad, so to tenderize things they leave meat out in the sun until it's stinking. Then they burn it a little bit in a fire—that's their idea of cooking, but all it does is burn the flies off and maybe crisp up the fly eggs. Their vegetables consist of things growing wild in the jungles, and they plant camotes. They'll make a clearing— they're really expert woodsmen; when they chop down a tree, they always direct its fall so that it knocks down three or four other trees—and fill it with camotes. Then, in three or four months, they'll come back from their hunting to dig the camotes up. If some other tribe has got in ahead of them, that starts another war.

Civilization has had some effect on them. They know what salt is. They come down to the coast to trade rattan for it. Then they even have lamps at night. The Manobos will wrap a long green leaf around a chunk of gutta-percha sap and have a light that burns for hours. The carbon crusts up on the gutta-percha every now and then and dims the light, but they just tap the carbon off and the light flares up bright again. But, civilization or not, when Baxter piled all his supplies in a dugout canoe and the canoe hit a log and he lost everything and he had to depend on the hill people, his health started to go down fast.

He finally made Hinatuan on the coast by about August 1, but he was in bad shape. The mayor and the chief of police invited him to dinner. They gave him a pretty fancy chow to make it last until late at night. Then the mayor took him over to show him something in a corner and the chief of police put a gun in his back and marched him off to jail. They wanted to do that late at night so none of the population would interfere. Their idea was to ingratiate themselves with the Japs, who had already been in Hinatuan twice on patrol.

They kept Long in jail for about a month, waiting for another Jap patrol to arrive. Several people offered to break him out of there, but Long was too tired and too sick and too discouraged. An orchestra came and stood outside his bars to play for him because he liked swing. They didn't play so good, but their hearts were in it. They offered to spring him, too. But he said no. What the hell was the use, he thought, of living in a tree and eating stinking meat. He'd take the prison chow.

The Japs finally arrived and brought him in slow stages to the municipal jail at Surigao. They treated him all right all the way up there. Long was parched for cigarettes. He swapped a Parker fountain pen with his guard for fifteen cigarettes and then he sat on his wooden bunk in his cell smoking up a storm. The cell was very dirty, but Long felt then it was going to be all right.

After a little while, Gidoka walked up. Gidoka had been a clerk for an American company in Manila and must have been other things on the side, because when the

Japs came in he immediately became a captain in the army. Maybe his treatment from the Americans hadn't been too good. Anyway, he was like most Japanese who have had anything to do with whites—he had a pathological hatred for them. Well, he walked right into Baxter's cell. He had two soldiers with him. They carried fixed bayonets and stood outside at first.

Gidoka was holding the fountain pen. "Was this yours?" he asked in perfect English.

"Why, yes. It isn't any more. I traded it with the guard for smokes."

"You are friendly with the guard?" That was what Gidoka was afraid of, I suppose, that if Long could make a deal for cigarettes, he could make a deal for other things.

"He seems all right. I can't talk his language and he can't talk mine, but he seems all right to me."

Gidoka stood looking at Baxter a minute. Then, without warning, he kicked Long in the groin and, when Long bent over, kicked him in the shins, then hit him in the face. The two guards with Gidoka opened the cell door and came inside quickly and stood there with their fixed bayonets.

Long didn't dare hit back. Gidoka was a big man for a Jap, about as tall as Long but much chunkier. I have seen him from hiding. He must weigh 190 pounds and none of it was fat. He beat Long for a long time. He kept talking as he did it. He'd knock Long to his knees. "That wasn't so good," he'd say and pick Long up by the front of his shirt. "Let's try it this way," he'd say and knock him all the way down. "There, that's good. That's better," and kick him as he lay there before picking him up and holding him and knocking him down again. The soldiers stood motionless with their fixed bayonets.

Finally all three went away. There was no explanation or warning, no saying, there, that'll teach you not to do that again. They just went away.

The next day Gidoka came again with two different soldiers. "How are you, Tom Baxter?" he asked. He was smoking a big cigar and looked pleasant and full, as if he had just eaten.

Long was lying on his bunk. He lifted up on his elbows, then swung one foot out of bed to get up. He was barefoot. His shoes had long since worn away. Gidoka grabbed the foot with his two hands and held the cigar against the instep. Long kept lunging back and forth while Gidoka rolled the burning cigar over the tender flesh of the instep. Finally Long, in one of his lunges, hit his head against the stone wall and knocked himself out.

This treatment kept up for two weeks. Gidoka concentrated mostly on the shins with his big army boots. Long still had scars there a year later. After the second day and no letup, Long searched his cell very carefully for something with which to kill Gidoka. He found a Schlitz beer can opener in the dust in a corner and a piece of quarter-inch pipe about four inches long. But he knew if he killed Gidoka, he would have to go, too, and Long wasn't ready to die yet.

The treatment stopped when Long was taken out during the day to work. He worked on concrete gun emplacements and digging foxholes. After a few days, the work stopped, but Gidoka's treatments did not resume.

Then on a Saturday afternoon, Long, looking out of his cell window, saw work begin on a gallows. There was a plaza back of the jail and Filipino laborers were putting it up there under the supervision of Japs. Sunday morning, Long found out the gallows was for him and another prisoner, a Filipino. The guard told him. He said the following Saturday was a day of fiesta and the Japs intended to celebrate it by hanging the two of them.

"Why?"

The guard shrugged. He did not know, but the execution was to be witnessed by the population and they were to draw a lesson from it.

Long waited all day for darkness. Those were as long hours as anybody ever has spent. His time for work was so limited. When darkness finally came, he went to work. He started in on the window bars with the beer can opener.

The bars were very thick and were made out of the hardest wood there is in the world—Bayong wood, which is much harder and denser than teak, or mahogany, or oak. He found out he had to knock out two of them. With only one, the opening wouldn't be wide enough for his head. The first thing, he rubbed a groove about two inches long with the sharp point of the beer opener. Then he worked with the curved end, scraping and extracting, first on the right side of the groove, then on the left. But the curve, even from both sides, didn't cover the whole width of the bar. It left a middle part untouched. Long sharpened the handle end of the opener on the stone floor and attacked the middle part with that, chipping it out. His idea was to hollow the two bars out, top and bottom, to keep the Japs from finding out during the day what he was up to. Then, when both bars were hollowed out, he'd snap them off and go.

He couldn't work steady. Two guards walked by outside intermittently all night long. Long's cell was on the ground floor and they could easily see if anything unusual was going on. But Long always saw them coming in time. His hands got blistered up in the first two hours of work, he worked so desperately, but he kept on until first light. Then he mixed the sawdust with dirt to hide it. He made a mud of dust to stuff into the holes he had worn in the bars. At dawn he'd run his hand over the bars unostentatiously to make sure the holes didn't show.

By dawn Tuesday morning, he had hollowed out the bottom part of the two bars. He made sure he had gone up to the rim without going all the way through by measuring with a splinter he chipped off his bunk. Then he found out the mistake he had made, working on the bottom first. The top was going to be much harder. He couldn't get the leverage there and he was all tired out now. He was panting as he worked. His panting sounded so loud in the quiet of the night that he was afraid it would give the alarm, but he couldn't hold it in. Jesus, it sounded just like whimpering and he couldn't hold it down. The muscles of his arms were so tired they were trembling all the time and his hands were all blistered up. Then he lost so much strength sharpening up the handle to chip the middle part of the bar.

Wednesday morning late, the Japs brought a Filipino kid in and threw him into the cell with Long. The kid seemed to have been through something. He went to sleep right away. Long didn't know what he was, whether he was a Jap plant or a fifth columnist or a boy without guts who would try to ingratiate himself with the Japs by turning Long in. But he didn't have time to waste. When darkness came, the kid was still asleep and Long went back to work.

About nine o'clock, he saw the kid lying still looking at him. Long was on a bench working at the top of the bars. He went over and put one hand on the kid's throat. Then he took his four inches of quarter-inch pipe that he had out of his pocket and held it before the kid's eyes.

"If you say a word," he said, "I am going to kill you with this."

He didn't even know whether the kid spoke English.

"Okay, okay," replied the kid. "Oh no, sir, I no talk."

"You are going to have escape with me." The kid looked at Long mutely. It was plain he didn't have the inclination. "If you stay after I'm gone, the Japs will kill you. That's too much temptation for you to talk. You are going to have to escape with me."

"Okay, okay. Oh, sir, yes, okay, sir."

"And if the Japs come in during the day to take you out of here for some reason, any reason, you had better make an excuse not to go. You had better be sick and without legs to walk, for, so help me God, if you try to get out of my sight I am going to kill you. I am going to knock your brains out with this pipe."

"Okay, okay."

Then Long put the boy to work. With his fresh arms, the thing went much faster. Long had bad, watchful moments the next day when the guard brought in their chow. He thought the kid might try to blurt out something, but the kid was all right.

Thursday night, nine o'clock, a typhoon blew up. There was a lot of rain with the wind. Then by ten o'clock it was all over, but there had been a failure in the power plant and the street lights didn't go on again. Long waited two minutes after the guards had passed outside, counting the seconds in his mind. He figured that would give him thirteen minutes. Then he snapped the bars off. The first one came clean. The second one took tugging by both of them together, and then it didn't break off all the way at the top. There were twines of wood there still holding. When it broke, it broke with a crack like a pistol shot. Long nearly fainted, but the wind was still loud in the trees and that must have covered the sound, for no one came.

Long motioned the kid out first with his pipe. There was grass about a foot high outside the window. The kid dropped soundlessly into it and lay down flat in it. He lay flat about ten seconds. Then he lifted his head and Long knew it was safe for him. He went through the bars, twisting the one back into place and sticking the other one back in to hide the fact of their escape as long as possible.

Just beyond the grass there was a path along which the guards walked. Then the grass began again and after that there was a border of ferns about three feet high. They ducked across the path and had to fall flat again. The guards were coming back. They fell flat under the fern border. It was really very bad for Long then. He thought something must have aroused the guards' suspicions to bring them back so fast. But they walked right by, two or three feet away, without stopping or hurrying, just sauntered along, and the darkness there, because there were no street lights, helped to keep everything looking normal.

Then Long kicked the kid to signal him, they didn't dare talk, and they lit out for the beach. At the beach they felt safe. They ran along it, looking to steal a banca or baroto to sail east where there would be jungle to hide in. Then Long saw the heelmarks of Jap army boots in the sand, three pairs of them. They were very clear and fresh because of the rain that had stopped a little while before. And in the darkness up ahead, Long made out the figures of them. They were a beach patrol and had turned around now and were coming towards them.

There was a banca there without sails. Long and the kid moved out into the water alongside the banca up to their heads. The wind was still kicking up flutters of water and that hid their splashes. When the Jap soldiers came abreast of the banca, Long and the kid moved stealthily around it to keep it between them and the soldiers.

About three hundred yards down the beach they found a baroto three-quarters full of water from the rain.

There were no paddles. The owner had taken them with him as a way to lock up his property. They scurried up and down the beach frantically, before the beach patrol could come back, and finally found a piece of bamboo about six feet long and maybe two inches in diameter. They broke it in two. The bamboo was green and they had to bend it back and forth many times before they could break off all the threads of it. There was a *bagool*— half a coconut shell—in the baroto to bail with, but they didn't dare waste more time. When they floated the baroto, it was more than half under the water. They paddled like crazy until they got out in the stream. Then one bailed, and the other paddled.

You can't paddle very well with round sticks two inches in diameter. In an hour and a half, they made about a half mile. Then Long found the current was taking them back to Surigao. It looked as if they were licked. There was no good country to hide in west of Surigao, until you got pretty far out. They turned the baroto around and paddled with the current. They passed the city about two in the morning and then, at first light, they beached the boat.

"Good-by, sir," the kid said. He knew he'd have a better chance without a white face around.

"Good-by," Long told him. He still had the pipe with him, but he felt what the hell was the use forcing the kid.

The kid took off by himself. Long didn't know what to do. His face, pulped up though it was still by Gidoka's ring, was like a flag, marking him wherever he went as an enemy of the Japs. Then along came an old man, a fisherman who had been out fishing all night. He had part of his catch on a string in his hand. He gasped and nearly dropped his catch when he saw Long. He could not talk any English, but he took Long to his hut, fed him, and covered him all over with copra sacks, and Long went right to sleep.

The old man lived all alone. Late in the afternoon, Long woke up. The old man was standing over him with a pistol. There was a ten-year-old boy alongside him. Long reached hopelessly for his pipe.

"I am my father's son, sir," the child said. The old

man had brought him along because he spoke English. "My brother, sir, in army. Before he will surrender, he give my father a pistol, sir. Sir, now it is to you."

It was a .32 and there were five rounds of ammunition with it. The old man took Long that night to a village down the coast. The whole village had buqweed except for one family.

Long stayed with this family about two weeks. The whole family worked in the fields all day except for one girl child, too young to work. She played around the house by herself and Long slept all day and all night. He hardly ever got out of bed, except for meals. But some fifth columnist found out he was there anyway and told the Japs, and the Jap-controlled Philippine Constabulary sent two men down to pick him up. They figured to cover the front and rear exits and holler for him to come out with his hands up. They knew his habits. They knew he had been beat up and slept all the time. So they just went at it easily and carelessly. They forgot about the little girl.

The little girl woke Long up. "Two men," she said. She was a wise child. She spoke in a very low tone. "They come here, sir."

"Go outside and play," Long told her. "Go quietly, but if they do not see you, run. Run as far away as you can, and play there and do not come back until it is time for supper."

It was then about two o'clock in the afternoon.

Long had his gun with him. He had learned to sleep with it cocked by his side. In all the years I have known him, I have never known him to sleep otherwise than with his gun cocked by his side. He went quietly to the window and saw a man standing there looking at him with mouth open with surprise.

There is no glass in the window of a nipa hut. It is just an empty space. The window came about halfway up on Long. He was standing with his gun down by his side. The man reached into his back pocket for his own gun. The hammer caught on the lining. He tugged at it and Long brought his gun up past the police badge on the man's chest and shot him dead between the eyes. Then he saw the second man running for the trees. The second man had been out back answering a call of nature. He ran with his pants around his ankles. In one hand he held his gun and with the other he was trying to pull up his pants. He didn't want to shoot until he had cover. Long shot and hit him in the side.

"Oi God, murder," the man screamed and spun all the way around and fell down. Long put another bullet into him. The man was still flopping. Long put a third bullet into him and waited. The man didn't flop any more. Long waited motionless for more than five minutes. He still had one bullet left. He did not want to waste it. After a while he climbed cautiously out the window and went over to the man and saw he was dead.

Long got two more guns out of the deal. The first cop had had a police positive .38 with six bullets. The second had had one of those bulldog revolvers, a .45, with six rounds in it and three more in his pocket. Now Long had three guns and sixteen bullets for them, and with these he started his own guerrilla army.

Bamboo telegraph usually brought word to one American of the existence of another. When they heard, they naturally started out for each other. In this way, Long Tom Baxter hooked up with Gordon Smith, who had been a cook in the army air corps, and Dutch Geysen, a character not even Joseph Conrad would have dared invent. Dutch is dead now, I am pretty sure, but in his time he had done everything a man could do running in sail and steam between Chile and the Orient, had learned all the languages there are, pretty near, from Russian to Mandarin, French, Visayan, Portuguese, and had been in every trade from mining to running slaves for rich Chinese.

He was a man with style, too. I remember when he decided once a fifth columnist was too dangerous to be let alone. He went to the man's wife. "Margherita," he said, "where is your husband?"

"In the fields with the carabao."

"Margherita, your husband is a bad man and I am going to kill him."

"Oh no, sir." She ran after Dutch to the road. "He is not bad. He is just weak."

"To be weak in times like nowadays, Margherita—that is very bad."

"If you kill him, I will have the world on your head."

"Margherita, when I kill a Jap lover, the world is by my side, steadying my hand."

He found the man walking home by the side of his carabao. He walked up to him quietly. "I am going to kill you," he said in an even voice and raised his pistol and shot him dead. Then he slung him over the carabao and brought the body back to the man's wife. She screamed filth at him.

"Margherita," he told her, "he was a bad man. You are better without him."

Carabao

But this twenty-two- or three-year-old American boy, Long Tom Baxter, was good enough to make himself the leader over even a man like that. They went up to the Mindanao mother lode mine and got a piece of iron Shelby tubing about eight inches long and grooved it with a file so that it would fragmentate when it exploded. They worked two sticks of dynamite into it, that they found in the mine, a cap and a fuse, and then plugged the tubing at each end with threaded iron stoppers. They left about two inches of fuse outside.

Then they went down to Malamono, where about twenty Japs were using the schoolhouse as a barracks. Geysen and Gordon Smith stayed on a hill there to give protective fire, and Baxter sneaked through tall grass there to an outhouse just behind the school building. They came at four o'clock, figuring to catch the Japs at chow.

The sweat from the excitement of working his way up to the outhouse had soaked through the scratch paper on Baxter's matchbox and for a long time he couldn't get a match to light. But he blew and fanned and finally a match lit and the fuse began to sputter. He held it in his hands a second or so, listening to the splutter and the Japs chattering inside the building, then heaved it straight-arm towards the window. It nearly missed. It went in just below the top.

"After that," Baxter told me, "nothing happened. I was running like hell. Then I looked back. The sides of the school building seemed to bulge a little. It bulged and snapped back and then things started flying through the clapboard walls."

There were seven or eight Japs late for chow. They saw Baxter running up the hill. He couldn't run very well at the time because his legs were still sore from Gidoka's boots. They threw a blast at him. He was wearing a great big straw hat to keep the sun out of his eyes and give his eyes a chance to heal from the beating they had taken in prison. When he fell flat, the brim of the hat hit and turned sideways on his head. A Jap bullet took the hat right off his head, the rope tied around his chin to hold the hat on pulling out through the straw.

Dutch and Gordon Smith lit out without firing a shot to cover Long. He had to zigzag away all by himself. Maybe that was why he was leader.

13

But the technician type of man that I was stayed in his little Lotos world, plucking the days as if they were daisy petals telling whether life loved him or didn't.

We all had skin ulcers at first. We wore makeshift clothes and none of us had shoes. Our skin would be scratched, and because there were no medicines or bandages the scratch would fester into an ulcer. There was a time when I thought Oscar Smith would lose a foot or die, the ulcer on it was so bad. But a dog saved him. A dog saved me, too. It started to lick the ulcer. At first I was going to kick it away, but an old Filipino fisherman there said "Ayaw-na" (never mind). The dog licked the wound clean. We kept the dog around two or three days and he cured up both of us, just with his tongue. After that we had the cure and the ulcers never again got a start on us.

Only a few of the boys grew beards. I didn't because it was hard enough anyway—dressed as I was, in rags and without shoes—to tell me from a bamboo American. I found a barber to shave me. He had a nicked-up razor and a piece of wood to sharpen it on. He'd wipe the razor on his hand and pants and go to work. There was no such luxury as soap. I got along for almost a year without any soap, just bathing every day in the sea. The barber shaved me for six months without ever charging me. It was painful, but less painful than appearing altogether like a bum would have been.

I tried to keep the men away from the bad native girls. Every barrio had its one or two like that, not professionals as far as Americans were concerned but sort of semi-pros. I appealed to the men at first on the grounds that as American soldiers they had a position to uphold. But the idea I got from them was to tie that one outside. Talking to them about the fine girls waiting for them back home worked better.

There were plenty of parties to pass the time, and I had my book to write about the PT boats. The Filipinos throw more parties than any other people in the world. There would always be drinks, a native booze called tuba. There are no drunkards in the Philippines on account of tuba. It tastes so bad. It is drawn from the palm tree. One of the fronds of a palm tree has on it a little bunch of a berry-looking sort of thing, instead of leaves. The Filipinos first chop all the coconuts off the tree. Then they train this frond for about two weeks until it hangs straight down. Then twice a day, in the morning and evening, they cut a thin sliver off the end and let the milk or sap bleed into a small bamboo tub. Pulverized tanbark from a mangrove tree is added as a fermenter and disinfectant, and the result is an 8.6 per cent kick. At the better parties, they shake up a pretty fair cocktail out of tuba by adding eggs, chocolate, and sugar. Filipinos can't say cocktail easily so they call it coetail or more generally cotare.

Filipino dances are always conducted in a blaze of light. There is none of this soft, romantic lighting going on. That would be too seductive. The girls sit on one side of the room with their chaperons, the boys on the other. When the band starts up, the boys make a rush for the girls. It's always first come, first served, and there are never any wallflowers. Filipino people are most friendly. They wouldn't think of hurting a girl's feelings by standing around and not dancing with her just because she happens not to be pretty.

Then, when the band stops, the girls rush right back to their chairs, and the boys go back to theirs. There is no mixing if the band isn't playing. The lights blew out frequently in those country dances because all they had was big kerosene lamps. When they do, the chaperons rush out into the middle of the floor and snatch their girls away.

Filipino girls can't be handled the way American girls are. Life is very strict for them, but there is a way around it. There is a way around everything and I have found out that most people, wherever they start from and however they travel, generally wind up doing the same things. But the boys were pretty well stymied at first. They'd dance with a girl, find out they liked her, and then they couldn't talk to her if the band stopped.

If you told a girl she was beautiful, she would say, "Oh, sir, you despise me, sir, you flatter me, sir. Sir, I do not like this. I am unaccustomed to it, sir."

And there you were, wondering what the hell had you done.

An American old-timer finally put the boys wise. He had seventeen kids and was married. He made four million pesos out of the war. But the Japs took it all away and killed one of his sons.

It seems the idea was there must be an in-between man. If a fellow sees a girl he likes, he doesn't look at her or touch her or try to talk to her. He may give her an occasional smile, but that's all. Then he finds her father's best friend, and invites him for a drink.

"These are hard times now," you say, "and I do not have a companion to solace the hours of my night, sir. I am very lonely."

He agrees times are hard and are even harder when the nighttimes are lonely. After that, the subject of the girl is broached.

"She is so beautiful. I really feel for her in my heart. She is as beautiful as the flowers in church. Do you think you could arrange it so that her father will smile on me?"

"Oh no. No, no, no." The answer is always no. "He is a good friend of mine and I know it is impossible for his daughter. You aim too high."

Then you buy the big man—as he is called—a demijohn of tuba, four and a half gallons. You present him with ten or twenty pesos. "Will you please entertain her father for me with this?"

The in-betweener and the girl's old man then get down to cases.

"He is an American. You know how Americans are. They do not act in our way, but he is a marvelous fellow."

"But it is impossible!"

However, the old man is still in there, listening.

You wind up finally buying two or three more demijohns of the tuba and having a dinner at their house. Nothing is ever mentioned of what is in everybody's mind, but after that it is all set—provided the girl is willing. Generally, she is. After all, she has what amounts to a go-ahead from her old man, and he can wave his hands and say, "Love, ah love, who can stand against love?"

The point is, you haven't gone over the old man's head. You've preserved propriety and shown respect. The Filipinos are a chaste Catholic people, but they are broadminded, too. They say a man will get sick or turn bad if he doesn't have a woman sometimes. Besides, they want mestizo kids. The Spaniards have been top of the heap out there for centuries. We think anybody with a drop of black blood is black. That seems very funny to them. They think anybody with a drop of white blood is white.

In the Philippines the word "lady" describes any unmarried girl. When a girl marries, she loses the title.

"Oh no, sir, I am no lady, sir. I have a husband."

The islands may very well be the genesis of that old gag—that was no lady, that was my wife. But do not hold that against them. When an American visited a girl in her father's house, she remained a lady.

We had a New Year's Eve party. It was, I think, about the last of the parties I attended. I had finished my book by now, and besides I kept thinking of Curly and how her aunt had promised to hide me out in Malitbog. Bancas plied back and forth to Malitbog every now and then, and I heard the Japs were there in small force, but not figuring to stay.

A woman high up in local society gave this party. She was Filipino-Chinese-Spanish and seemed to have made money out of every branch of the family tree. It was a dinner party on plates and tablecloth with fifteen courses— lichon, Chinese, Filipino, and Spanish dishes, beautiful fruit salads with pineapple, mangoes and papayas and coconuts shredded up and sugared. Our hostess got very angry first off because the guests stole her spoons. She said she was going to have all future parties in the afternoon because it was too easy for the guests to stick the silver in their pockets at night.

It was a formal party. Everybody wore shoes except the Americans. It was known that the Americans had come by their bare feet patriotically and they were excused. All the *dalagas* and beautiful girls were there, dressed in the very best they had. Some had nice silk dresses and some even had high-heeled shoes. Their hair was all curled. All the hair-curling places up and down the coast had been busy for three weeks before New Year's Eve. Some of the poorer girls would just take a nail and piece of tin to curl their hair. They'd wrap a strand of hair around the nail, then clamp it with the tin. Their mothers would tip a hot flatiron against the tin. Sometimes the iron would slip. There was always a smell of scorched hair around a formal Filipino party. They had something they called "medicine," too, "hair medicine." It put a permanent wave to their hair. There was a whole floorful of permanent waves for this party.

After dinner, there was a dance. The orchestra was led by a wonderful little screwball, a natural comedian with whom I lived a long time. He didn't give a damn about the Japs. He had more guts than forty guerrillas, even the guerrillas I worked with later. He was the drummer as well as the leader. He owned the only drum for two hundred kilometers up and down the coast. The drum made the orchestra neutral territory when a fight started. Nobody wanted to risk breaking it. The Filipinos never fight at their parties, but the Americans always do. That was an extra attraction added by our boys. A fellow who wanted sanctuary in a fight just had to run and stand by the drum.

My friend had worked up a swell little dance band. They used to listen to what American records they could find and take their music and orchestrations off that. They could play anything ten years old darn good. They had worked up a little skit for their leader. He'd step out among the dancers and wander around, directing the orchestra by waving one of those wire brushes that they use on snare drums. The brush had a little ring on it. If you pulled it up, it would fold tight into a kind of stick. If you let it down, it would flare out into a brush again. He'd make believe he was mixed up and start directing a dancing couple with the brush squeezed into a stick. It was very funny. I've seen him do it many times, but it always seemed very funny to me. Then he'd start shaking his foot in a jitterbug step and the orchestra would make believe *it* was mixed up and follow the rhythm of his foot instead of the stick.

"No, no," he'd scream, "the stick, not the foot."

He'd wave the stick excitedly, which would make the orchestra play all excitedly and mixed up. Well, by that time everybody was laughing so much the tears would be running down their faces, but the orchestra would look very serious and as if it was trying very hard to do the right thing. Then, when things got smooth again, he would pull the ring down and the stick would flare into a brush and he'd use it for a fan. That was always the funniest part. He'd put the stupidest grin on his face. The orchestra would follow the rhythm of the fan, all wavering and broken up.

Maybe it doesn't read funny, but it was very funny when my friend did it.

Oh, I liked him very much. He was the poorest man in the neighborhood, but neither he nor his wife would hear of my going. They really took on as if it would wound them and I stayed with them rather than with the rich people around there.

There were five demijohns, about twenty-three gallons, of cotare. The woman had bought out the whole town to get the chocolate to make it. There must have been two hundred eggs in it. The Americans knew our hostess didn't like to see them get too drunk. She had had unhappy experiences before. So they took their cotares and lined them up behind the flowers on a table where she couldn't see how many they were having. They picked the table closest to the girls. Then, when I got the nod from my drummer friend that the orchestra was starting, we'd have a head start over the local boys. We'd rush over and block the other boys off and that way get first pick of the girls.

Franky Divino was there. He had been a kid with a carnival for five years and then he went with the Barnum and Bailey circus. He got only to the eighth grade in school. He thinks he doesn't know anything about anything, but he is a master storyteller. He looks like he should wear a derby hat and carry a cane and walk down the boardwalk in checked pants instead of being a refugee from a broken-down American Army that took a real pasting from an army that was just too much for it to handle. He had been in the air corps and had come over the mountains to us with Johnny Colota, a boy from New York City.

Franky didn't dance. Girls embarrassed him. He said he didn't know what to do with a nice girl, only a bad one.

"You do the same thing," we told him.

"Nuts," he said, "you're just trying to horse me up."

"No," we told him, "that's on the level. Just dance and press up against them. They like it the same as anybody else."

"Brother," he said, "tell me more."

After he had danced, he came back all excited: "How long has this been going on?"

"Why, Franky," we told him, "what do you think makes nice girls nice?"

He took to being a regular bearcat on the dance floor. He didn't miss a dance.

"You're doing fine, Franky," we told him.

Then one of the fellows spoiled it. "After all, there is a limit," he said, "you ought to let them keep their clothes on at least."

Franky hadn't been as bad as most, but he turned all colors. He wouldn't dance any more that night, and I don't think he ever danced again.

For midnight, Jimmy Hardman asked the mayor to lend him his gun to fire one shot out the window. Jimmy was an American mestizo. He had been lightweight boxing champion of the Orient until the war.

"Jeemy, wan shot okay, two shots bad because it's my bullets."

"Okay, wan shot."

Jimmy staggered over to the window and bam! bam! bam! bam! bam! bam! he emptied the whole gun into the night.

"Jeemy, my God, my bullets!" shouted the mayor.

Bullets were a very scarce item in town. The guerrillas grabbed all they could find.

"No more bullets?" said Jimmy. "Then I sleep."

"Why you no think of that before?" cried the mayor.

Then the orchestra wanted to go home, but McCagley, who had some money he had won in poker, said he would pay five pesos if they played until dawn. Our hostess began to look worried.

McCagley went over to the mayor. There is something about McCagley's face when he is happy with cotare that makes you think he is angry. I don't know what it is, but he looks over his head in a fight. Hardman, waking up, took one look at McCagley walking over to the mayor and got up to help him.

"Sit down," said Divino.

He didn't want there to be a fight.

"Nobody's going to . . ."

"Sit down. There's no fight."

"Not unless I'm in on it."

Hardman cocked his fists and started to push past Divino, so Franky socked him to cool him off. He knocked the champ cold for about five minutes. St John came busting over to see what had happened. Somebody hit him. Then the fight started.

The fight boiled up all over the place. It looked for a time as if people were going to come out through the sides of the house. Then the police came in and all the Americans jumped on them, resenting the intrusion. An old man there got the women shrieking into the bedroom. The cops brandished pistols and the women lay in their silk dresses on the dirty floor shrieking. They wanted to get where, if there was any firing, they wouldn't get hurt. The mayor was running around yelling "Stop! Stop!" to the cops and "Stop! Stop!" to the Americans, everybody was throwing a punch at everybody else, and our hostess was having a cat fit.

There were people trying to get out of the house, but Americans stood at the door punching anybody who made a break. Stay and take your punishment until we find out who the guilty are, that was their idea. The Filipinos build their houses so that every time there is an addition to the family, they can make an addition to the house. Each wall has a door in it to facilitate tacking on an extra room. Three fellows grabbed open one of those doors there and ran on through it before finding out there was no room tacked on. The door was just a high step to nowhere. On the way down one of the boys grabbed a big stone water pitcher to stop himself from falling. It landed on him and knocked him cold for an hour.

Divino kept running around, shouting, "There was no fight. There was no fight." If there wasn't, appearances were sure deceiving. He'd pull a guy around and yell at him, "You damn fool, there was no fight." Then the guy would clip him for pulling him like that and Divino would clip him back.

Finally he had enough people convinced there had been no fight in the first place. Then the whole thing simmered down and stopped. People were shaking hands all around. This always puzzled the Filipinos. They couldn't understand why Americans shook hands after a fight, but then they couldn't understand either why there should have been a fight at all.

"Christ," a fellow looked around at the wreckage, "it looks like the Japs been here."

Somebody heard him. "The Japs," he cried and broke for the door.

Fellows poured out of every opening. They jumped through windows and ran out doors and through the phony door in the wall, too. "There are no Japs," I wailed after them, but they wouldn't stop. For a long time you could hear the thudding of them and the crashing as they fled in separate ways to the jungle.

Then St. John and myself and our hostess were all that was left of the party. There was still some cotare and we didn't want it to go to waste.

"The party started so nicely." Our hostess sighed.

"It was good all the way through. Everybody had a fine time."

"It was a shame about the fight," said St. John.

"No, that was good, too. It gave everybody a chance to let off steam."

"Americans always have so much steam," our hostess said unhappily.

I think it was a few days later that a Jap plane came over the hut where we were staying. He came low and slow and looked so agonizingly full of power. I hit for under the hut in case he should strafe, but Pierson, who had the malaria at the time, lost his head.

"Come on down and fight with your fists, you Jap bastard!" he screamed and shook his fist at the plane.

The plane passed over slowly, then circled low and slow and came back for another look.

"Hit the deck," I shouted, "he's going to let you have it."

"The bastard! The no-good bastard!" He stood there with legs spraddled, all windy with fever, and shaking his fist. "I'll spot you a knife against my fists, you Jap bastard."

The Jap passed on slowly. He didn't fire, but Pierson didn't duck.

After that I decided it was time to move. We were all beginning to come unraveled down there in Lotos land.

14

I headed for Malitbog first. I heard the Japs had left and I wanted to see Curly. Malitbog is on Sogod Bay—pronounced so good—on the southern coast of Leyte. As soon as I got ashore, they told me an American colonel was there with his army.

It turned out to be Colonel Morgan. He was an American mestizo, formerly in the Philippine Constabulary, who had burned a big lumber camp at Columbugan rather than let the Japs have it, and then had joined up with Col. Wendell Fertig. Fertig, he said, had been a mining engineer on the islands before going into the U. S. Army to fight the war. After the surrender, he had been assigned by General MacArthur to handle the guerrilla activities on Mindanao. Morgan explained he was now moving around for Fertig trying to get the guerrillas everywhere to unify in separate military departments. When they did unify, they would get recognition from MacArthur, and aid. But no recognition as long as the monkey business kept up.

"It's a regular on-the-level war then?"

"It's going to be."

That was his promise.

"People who mean business are the only ones who have a chance. They are the ones who will unify, form a military department, and get recognition and aid. When the recognition comes, the people will treat the others as bandits."

It looked good to me right away. Anyway, it looked better than anything I had seen before. But I wanted to sleep on it awhile. The men with Morgan didn't look any different from any of the others who called themselves guerrillas. There were sixty of them. That Morgan wasn't taking chances with the Japs or any disgruntled guerrillista leader. But his soldiers were a dirty, ragged, unshaven, cutthroat-seeming crew.

However, when Morgan left Malitbog, he and his army sailed in three big, beautiful bancas. It looked like a Pacific Fleet task force to me.

I went to the home of the Escanos to find Curly. Teting was there, and Loling. She was all recovered from the cesarian operation she had had in Tacloban when the Japs came in. The Escano home was called "the Casa." It was a beautiful estate with thirty rooms, most of them commanding views of Sogod Bay. American officers had been quartered there in the 1898 war. The plumbing was blessedly perfect—showers, flush toilets, porcelain tubs, hot and cold running water. There was a grand piano, several radios, carpets, tapestries. The whole house was furnished in magnificent style and had a large staff of servants. It was the kind of place where you just automatically dress for dinner. When I saw it, I didn't want to go in. I was in rags. I felt like scraping my bare feet on the mat before knocking, but they made me feel like visiting royalty.

Curly wasn't there. She was living with her family on another island, where there was a garrison of about five thousand Japs. That sure locked her away from any American. Her cousin, Fermin, said he was going over to see her soon, so I asked if he'd mind taking a letter.

I wrote Curly, recalling myself to her and saying, "If you're not doing anything, why don't you visit your cousins? I'll probably still be here and we'll talk over the good old days."

Fermin brought back her answer later, that she remembered me very well and was delighted I was well and safe, that her father did not want to let her travel to Leyte at the moment, but that she had got a promise from him that she could make the next trip back with Fermin. He traveled back and forth fairly often. With the letter were regular American cigarettes and a bottle of Scotch whisky.

But by that time I had already gone to see Colonel Kangleon and had undertaken my first mission as a guerrilla.

Col. Ruperto Kangleon had been in the Filipino Army for twenty-seven years. He was the first native to be made divisional commander by MacArthur. He was an important figure in Leyte as a local boy who had made good in the big cities to the north. After the defeat, he had surrendered to the Japanese with his unit. Later, aided by guerrillas, he had managed to escape from the concentration camp and make his way back to the hills of southern Leyte. His escape caused a great sensation. It gave him a head start over any other guerrilla, but then his lifetime had, too.

Kangleon was a tired, sick old man from his escape when I saw him. He was wiry and leather-faced, but under the military barbering he gave his words and his bearing there was sickness and discouragement and terrible fatigue. He was living with his wife and, I think, five children then (he kept adding one or twins almost every year). They had a very clean little house with shiny white bamboo floors. It was hidden in the hills. Nobody could come along the road to it without being stopped by men who hid in the bushes and held you until the colonel had agreed to see you.

The bamboo of the house's flooring was laid in strips with a quarter-inch space between for ventilation and utility. The cracks made sweeping easy. His home was divided into four rooms with a lean-to kitchen which had one of those native sandbox stoves. The stove is just an ordinary box of sand. Wood is burned in the sand and iron tripods are placed on it to hold the pots above the fire. Over the stove is a rack on which green wood is placed to dry.

These were the headquarters of the Leyte guerrillas—such as they were at the time. It represented quite a comedown for the colonel and Mrs. Kangleon. They both took it very well. There was no self-pity in either of them. Mrs. Kangleon is a large woman, considerably larger than her husband, and wonderfully feminine. She is a typical Filipina, demure, very pleasant, and even-tempered. There is never any excitement around her. Everything runs smoothly and without crises. She had two muchachas to help her, but she ran the house and liked to do things herself.

Later on, the Japs raided the house. They captured the colonel's brother and three of the children. Mrs. Kangleon had to go out the back, carrying her baby and nothing else. But when she got into a new house, it wasn't an hour before everything was running just as smoothly as if nothing had happened. If she wept, she wept alone or in the privacy of her husband's arms.

Although Colonel Kangleon was boss of a guerrilla band, there was no looting where he was. That was the first thing that impressed me about him. He supported himself the best he could. He tended his farm there at the time—some rice, bananas, and a potful of vegetables, all for home consumption. He raised chickens and pigs for home consumption, too. For amusement, he had a parrot. He kept trying to make it talk, but it never would say anything you could recognize as a word.

To get money he had built himself a soap factory. This consisted primarily of a wooden wheel and handle with a rope belt to a spindle that was mounted in a bracket. The spindle had a pulley on one side of the bearing and on the other side a scraper of the fruit-juicer variety. The scraper was used to extract and shred the meat of coconuts. Then the shreds were boiled and the coconut oil floated to the surface. After the water boiled off, an extract of hardwood ash was added to it. The extract was made by running sea water through the ash. The ash and the oil were then stirred and boiled together. It thickened, hardened, and became soap. It wasn't very good soap, but it was better than none, and the colonel cut it into one and one-eighth pound cakes and sold them for forty centavos apiece—twenty cents. The guards let customers come up to the house to buy.

When I came in on him that first time, a soldier was turning the wheel and the colonel was holding coconut shells to the juicer.

I introduced myself as an officer in the United States Navy. He said he had heard of me from other Americans.

Then we discussed for a long time the problems of guerrilla organization—how to unify in order to get recognition and aid, how to live until the aid arrived without preying on the people.

"The Japs have all withdrawn from southern Leyte," he said. "But hunger is the first enemy of any army.

"Since there are no Japs," he said then, "it is a good time to organize and grow strong. While the cat is away, we may play. But since there are no Japs, we have nothing to organize with. If they were here, we could call on them in surprise for guns and supplies."

I came away from there with a mission. He had sent two people to try to contact Colonel Fertig. They both had disappeared without trace. I offered to be the third to try.

"Then you can go to work for me, if you'd like that."

"I'd like it fine."

I preferred to work on Leyte rather than Mindanao because that would give me a chance to see Curly sometime.

15

In a Caba-Caba (small banca) with forty pesos and a Smith and Wesson revolver given me by Colonel Kangleon I traveled into a world I had never known existed, a world that lived nearly unknown except to those directly concerned.

At first unfavorable winds blew me off course. Then I met an American Jesuit priest who warned me against the direct route to Colonel Fertig. The Japs, he said, had been overtaking bancas with their launches and removing cargo and crews. He recommended I see Colonel McLish first.

Smith and Wesson .38

So I sailed again and had luck about the Japs, didn't even see any, and found the colonel very easily, just by asking natives. When I got to him—oh, it was like suddenly hearing Benny Goodman after trying to fool yourself with a ukulele for a long time. Here was music. Here was the business, a guerrilla outfit with that fine feeling of controlled power Americans give anything they're in. There was a whole herd of Americans, both army and navy—Major Childress, Ed Dyess, survivor of the death march, Mike Dobervitch, who had also escaped from Davao Penal Colony, Long Tom Baxter, Gordon Smith, Mooney, who had been Colin Kelly's radioman on the raid on the *Haruna,* Captain Knortz, an air corps enlisted man who had earned his commission in the field, big Dick Lang, air corps mechanic who was 6 feet, 3 inches and weighed 235 pounds, Lieutenants Marshall and Spielman, who had been on the death march with Dyess, McCoy, Mellnick, Schaeffer, and the rest of those—all of whom had made their way safely to guerrilla land.

There was no looting civilians for those boys, no sir. They had an orchestra to raise money. It had formerly played in a big night club in Cebu. They had inducted the whole works, men and instruments, into the guerrilla army. Then the guerrilla army had the best band west of Ford Island, Pearl Harbor. There was a dance every night, admission 50 centavos. The natives would come for miles because this was a real hot band. It seems a funny way to run an army's procurement system, but it is no funnier than the shows they give in the United States to sell War Bonds.

Colonel McLish said he would be leaving soon for G.H.Q., as he called the house in which Fertig hid, and would be glad to take me. We put out in the launch *Rosalia,* a very fine motorboat captured from the Japanese in a battle at Butuan.

"We start small," the colonel told me. "Armies fight to stab an enemy country's heart. That means, generally, take the capital. But to take the capital you have to destroy their army. To destroy their army, you have first to take the road nexuses behind them so that they can't run away. To do that you must get through them. To get through them, you must take high ground. To take high ground, you must have an army. To have an army, you must have men. To have men, you must have supplies. That's where we're starting—all the way back of the goal posts. Our present battles are for supplies. We don't even fight for our lives. That would waste bullets. We just run for them. But we fight Japs for supplies. *Ipso facto,* the *Rosalia.*"

The *Rosalia* looked very *ipso* to me and even more *facto.* Colonel McLish put me in charge. "When I joined the army," he declared, "the navy said, 'We'll take you there.' Okay, boy, take me." I checked speed and course and, wanting to make Misamis City at 0530 hours in the morning, got under way at three in the afternoon. Ed Dyess came along, ten soldiers, and the regular boat crew.

It was fine fun.

About four o'clock in the morning, we were going along with a good, smooth gush, the two lookouts on the bow looking alert and satisfactorily dim when suddenly their black bodies turned bright pearly gray. A searchlight was on them, a big one, a destroyer searchlight.

I called for more speed. We had been making six knots. "Can you give me more?" I asked the engineer.

"Oh, okay, sir," he replied, "plenty more."

Ed Dyess and McLish came alongside me. I deployed the ten soldiers along the boat, and warned them not to fire. You never can tell what the army will fire at with their rifles.

"Steady as you go," I told the helmsman.

The engines were turning over faster. You could feel them. Then I realized that what you could feel was the clutch slipping. We were down to two or three knots.

"Belay that," I told the engineer. "Go ahead and make your six knots."

"Oh, okay, sir."

The searchlight swung to left of us and rambled there, then to right of us and rambled there. Then, it went out. I could make out the destroyer in the gloom now. It was very near. After two or three minutes, the searchlight came on again. It walked sweeping towards us across the sea.

"Hard right." I yelled it in a very loud voice.

"Sh-sh, not so much English around here," whispered Dyess.

The launch came around to the right.

"Steady as you go," I said in a lower tone, then asked Dyess, "How do you say that Visayan way, boy?"

The light was full on us. It made us look a bleached-out kind of bluish green. I could see by Ed's face he didn't feel much like grinning, but he grinned at me.

We headed right for the beach. I knew what I was doing. We were off the point four miles above Jimenes, Occidental Misamis. There is a reef there that extends out from shore for more than a mile. At low tide, you can walk all the way out on it. At high tide, the *Rosalia*—which had plied the Butuan River originally—could go right in while a ship couldn't follow us. We ran up to within twenty yards of the beach, stopped, backed down one, stopped again and threw over the hook.

"Hit the beach," I said.

The Filipinos didn't want to go. They had fought hard for the *Rosalia*. They didn't want to part with it.

I brought up my gun. "Get ashore," I said. "Nobody is kidding around here. Not that destroyer out there, either."

The Filipinos took all their stuff. The engineer removed the injectors from the Diesel engines. The whole thing went quite nicely. The ship didn't fire a shot at us and the water to wade in wasn't over our knees.

Colonel McLish made for the hills to see what was going on. I wanted to burn the boat, but he said no, to wait and see what was happening. I deployed the ten soldiers along the beach so that if the destroyer sent a landing party we could make an answer. Then a runner came down from the colonel with orders to join him on the double. By then it was dawn. I could make out that the night's "destroyer" was a five-hundred- to seven-hundred-ton cargo vessel, the kind the Japs use for landings. But it was too late to burn the *Rosalia*. The cargo vessel had machine guns and pom-poms and she was in close enough to lather anybody who showed his head.

The runner led us to Colonel McLish. He had found an old man up early in his rice paddies. "Are there any Japs?" he had asked.

"No, no people here at all."

The colonel had gone on. Ten minutes later the old man, breathless, had caught up with him.

"Forgive me," he said, "I did not recognize you at first as on our side." The old man had puzzled the whole thing out with his slow mind. White face is not Japanese face, but is not Filipino face either. If not Filipino, then Japanese. But if white, then not Japanese either. Must be American. It had taken him four or five minutes to work this out. Then he had pushed his old bones as fast as they would go. He was breathing painfully when he arrived and gasping as he talked. "There many *Hapons* (Japanese) above where you go."

So McLish had sat where he was until we joined him. We began working through rice paddies. It was like a nightmare there. Everything was so quiet. We felt in our minds as if things should be blowing up, as if there should be shots and pursuit and grappling, but there was only quiet and the whicker and puddling and whisper-whisper of jungle clearings and jungle.

A woman came running down a road. "Hapons!" she cried. "Hapons coming!" and ran on.

A platoon of Jap soldiers passed us while we crouched low. They made a scuffling sound as they walked. Their equipment creaked and scraped. They were deployed in a skirmish line. We didn't fire our ten rifles at them. We didn't know what was ahead or behind them or where to run away from where we were. They padded past us like figures in a dream.

Then a Zeke came over and began strafing the *Rosalia* and the beach behind it. The passionate, riveting sound tore at our minds. Not a shot was fired at the plane. Oh, no. We were mice in a hole. Mice don't bite back at what's biting them.

The Japs had landed in every place in the province, up and down each side of the peninsula, in one operation, a swoop to catch the guerrillas off guard and get their supplies before they could haul them away. It was a painful blow. The Japs knew every last detail of where to go. Fertig had been using widely scattered hill houses as storage dumps. Where these were inaccessible to their troops, the Japs sent airplanes. The airplanes made few

"Zeke"

mistakes. They'd pick the right house out of a cluster of them and work over it until they had leveled it or set it on fire. In two days, the whole quartermaster department was in ashes.

But they didn't get Fertig, and they got very few of his people. They got all the launches and all transport, but not people. When we finally found Fertig, he had established new headquarters in a place identical with the old one—just an ordinary hill house on stilts. Very few people were allowed up there. Most business was done at an outpost that guarded the approach to the headquarters. The idea of this was to prevent fifth columnists from finding out just which hill house was headquarters. They weren't so much afraid of enemy troops as of planes. There would be ample warning on troops, but they couldn't run out and hide every time a plane came over. They'd never get any business done.

Fertig kept the most mobile headquarters I have ever seen. It was the kind that he could jump through a window with and be off any time of the day or night it became necessary. He had a little suitcase in which he kept the maps and papers and codes necessary for daily business. All he had to do was take that up and go. His records, files, and other impedimenta were stored in holes in the ground. The holes were kept carefully covered. It was a curious filing system, but under the circumstances eminently practical.

By the time I arrived, Fertig was already in daily contact with "Souwespac," as General MacArthur's Southwest Pacific headquarters were called. Contact had been made in December, 1942. Robert C. Ball, an air corps man from Indiana, and William F. Konko and Stewart Willever, Jr., radio operators out of our PT squadron, had escaped the Japs and joined up with Fertig in the hills. "You're my signal corps," Fertig told them. They scrounged around and improvised and invented and did without and finally went on the air. It was strictly hambone, but it worked. It could send and it could receive.

They played their key a week, trying to get San Francisco. Day after day went by without an answer. They thought maybe their set didn't work. Each night, they'd take it down and put it together again. Then in the morning, there would still be no answer.

Then suddenly dots and dashes: A very much startled San Francisco was asking, who are you . . . and not believing it.

They had been using some old cylindrical encoding devices that Colonel Fertig had taken with him. They announced the setting up of a guerrilla organization. There was a delay then of about two days. Finally San Francisco suggested using another code.

Colonel Fertig had thought to bring the paraphernalia with him that you need for this system. The longer I knew Fertig, the more I saw that he had thought of in advance. He was a real businessman, a real executive. He had never been in the guerrilla business before, but he ran it as if it were a corporation—a shoestring corporation, but with all the shoestrings there could possibly be.

Then days went by, ten of them. The boys had a daily

signal from San Francisco, but no message. Then from the FBI, the army's G2, the Office of Naval Intelligence, and related bureaus came a message requesting identification data.

They weren't taking any chances. There was a chance the Japs had got Fertig's or Ball's dog tags and were using them to mislead MacArthur. There was a remote chance that one or the other or any two or three of the men named in the original message had gone over to the Japs and were working with them. But there was no chance all had and our intelligence people back home made security doubly secure by picking two names at random and requesting identifying information of the kind Japs could not torture out of prisoners unwilling to co-operate with them.

I delivered to Colonel Fertig a letter from Colonel Kangleon. We talked for about half a day straight of the problems involved in putting a guerrilla organization on a sound working basis in Leyte. There must first be unification, he said. With unification would come recognition. With recognition would come permission to establish a civil government in the name of Quezon. When you have a civil government, even if it's only governing twelve nipa huts and a tin outhouse, you can get permission to print money backed by Quezon's funds in Australia, and issue it. With money, you can organize an army.

"If you do things in that order," Fertig said, "you can't miss. Quezon will not be able to refuse, even if he should feel so inclined."

At the headquarters I met Lieutenant Commander Chick Parsons, who had come up as MacArthur's personal representative to the Philippines. Fertig and Parsons were a wonderful team. They were the Nimitz and MacArthur of our little frog-filled pond. What Fertig did to uphold the reputation of the United States Army for courage, efficiency, ingenuity, and dauntless resolve during a wretched time Parsons did to uphold the reputation of the United States Navy.

He dragooned me to work for the navy. "What we want out of you," he said, "is intelligence—a radio station in San Bernardino Straits above Samar and other radio stations around Samar and Leyte where they can watch Jap ship movements."

I couldn't say no.

16

We had to walk through five hundred kilometers of Japs before we could get where it would be safe for me to take a banca back to Leyte. It was very hard. I had never been fat, but I lost about thirty pounds. Towards the end I could feel my bones rubbing through my skin and hurting it. Our party consisted of Colonel McLish, the ten soldiers, and myself. We had with us two thousand rounds of .30-caliber ammunition and five large boxes of medical supplies. We had to stop in every town to get volunteer carriers to help us along to the next town. We walked with a Filipino scout going ahead, unarmed and looking as if he were a boy from the neighborhood out on an errand. Behind him came an advance party of four soldiers with rifles, then the main body with packs and equipment, and finally a rear guard. In case of anything suspicious, the scout would drop back to the advance party, and the advance party would sound a warning with a bojong. A bojong is a conch shell with a hole in it. Blowing through the hole produces a low, melancholy, far-reaching note that you can hold until it swells up the ears. There is a bojong bird that sounds just like it which makes it useful for warnings, but every time a bojong bird sounded off we thought, here it is, and ducked laboriously into the jungles. It slowed us up considerably. We had to send a runner up to contact the advance guard and find out if it was their bojong that we were hiding from or a bojong's bojong.

We tried to average twenty-five kilometers a day. After a while, my heart developed a sort of bubbling flutter. It wasn't anything the Japs had done, just fatigue. Dyess had had it, too. Everybody walking the jungle gets it sooner or later. It comes when you push yourself too hard, and goes away when you rest awhile. You lie down and it feels like a pump squishing and squashing in your chest. Then it goes away. Sometimes there is a fever with it, but that goes away, too.

Before leaving headquarters, Fertig gave me a present which made me feel as happy as anything that ever had happened to me before in my whole life. I remember when my mother had given me an automobile for my own, but not even that compared with this: GI shoes and two pairs of socks, two of them, mind you, a brand-new thick white towel out of navy small stores—oh, I can still smell the cleanness of it when I first put it on my face—two packages of razor blades, one prophylactic toothbrush, five packs of Lucky Strike cigarettes.

I was a new man. The shoes were hard to walk in at first. I had been barefoot so long. When you walk barefoot, you unconsciously grip the ground. I kept gripping the insides of the shoes, and I felt insecure and as if I were slipping. However, after a week it was just as if I had never been barefoot at all. The shoes were only one size too big for me. With the extra socks, they fit fine, and I wouldn't have parted with them for anything, even during those first days when I felt my feet were suffocating and that I was slipping and my feet were clutching at the insides of the shoes all the time like hands. After that, even at night in the jungle, I wouldn't go barefoot. It's easier to follow a path if you do. You brush your bare foot from side to side and feel for the broken grass or wood of a path. But I had shoes! It doesn't matter how ragged your clothes are as long as you have shoes. I had promised myself that if I ever did manage to get hold of a pair I'd polish them so that they'd make all the other shoes in the world look like worn-outs. Before leaving, I got some polish from a Chinese store and I polished my shoes every noon and every night and put a sheen on them every morning so that I could shave in them.

I remember that about the walk, the polishing of the shoes, and the setting of them in the crotch of a tree every morning and the looking in them to shave, the clammy, dragging feel of sweaty clothes, the salt sting of sweat running in my eyes, the sudden blessedly cool feeling of brook water breaking through my shoes and running fast and tickling like cool little mouse paws all over my feet at once, the nettles and the grasses of underbrush lashing the blood to the surface of the arms and legs, the dank musty-seeming odor of jungle, the dry smell of hill roads powdering into my nose like dust, and the squishing and squashing of my heart, and sweat and blisters and sweat on them, salting and burning them, and sweat making my hair feel like gobs of mud on my head, and the winds of typhoons throwing rain so hard the drops felt like bags of pebbles, and sweat running down on my lips, and balls of sweat rolling slowly down my back as if they were bugs crawling and the bojong sounding and a Jap armored column whisking by while we lay in the jungle, wondering sweatily, what are we doing here, how did Americans ever get into a world like this?

It was August 16 before I got back to Colonel Kangleon. He didn't recognize me at first. Bamboo telegraph had brought word to him I was dead. He didn't show much emotion. He is a stickler for military demeanor, but I could tell he was glad to see me. It meant he had made contact with Fertig.

17

The day before I reached Kangleon's headquarters there had been a pitched battle between his men and Miranda's. This Miranda was what is called in mixed company a picturesque character. His real name is supposed to have been Blasmeyer. He had been a second lieutenant in the Philippine Army at the start of the war. After the surrender he promoted himself to be general and started his own *borobo*—guerrilla force. He is a quick boy with a bolo, and his *borobo* thrived.

By August he was the only guerrilla leader in the Samar-Leyte area who had refused to join Kangleon. Kangleon had used threats on some, persuasion on others, but neither threats nor persuasion had worked on Miranda. He had his territory and nobody was going to be boss over him there.

There was a Captain de Gracia working for Kangleon. He went up to Baybay in Miranda's territory to see a girl and heard stories there about Miranda's activities that made him decide to try to hold the barrio. Kangleon agreed and sent troops to help him. On August 15, Miranda came out of the hills to take back "his" town. The van of his attack consisted of civilians into whose left hands he had pressed white flags and into whose right hands he had pressed spears. Then his troops came behind with their guns pointed at the backs of the civilians to make sure they would advance.

Kangleon's soldiers were weeping as they fired into the civilians. The battle lasted all day. About two hundred were killed in it. As I remember, eight of ours were killed and thirty captured. Towards evening, they got two .50-

.50-Cal. M.G. Ground Mount

caliber machine guns into the town and then our side retired, leaving Miranda still boss of his territory.

Miranda remained boss up there until December 6. Kangleon couldn't do anything about him because his men objected. Killing Japs was one thing. But killing Filipinos did not seem honorable to them nor glorious. In fact, the battle had precipitated something of a crisis in the ranks, and the first mission Kangleon gave me when I returned was to talk to his men and explain the new setup.

There were about twenty-five officers at the meeting, most of them sullen and with a show-me attitude. "First," I said, "you are no longer considered deserters." This had been rankling them, the fact that they hadn't surrendered with their units technically making them deserters. "Guerrilla warfare is a recognized form of international war. I just got in on the dope from Southwest Pacific.

"Second, unification is an essential. Without unification, there cannot be recognition. How can they, sitting thousands of miles away, tell who is in this thing to be a pirate and who is in it to win the war? No, there must be one outfit. And without recognition, there cannot be aid. The people who stand against us in this are standing with the Japs.

"Third, I've just got permission for us to have a civil government that will print money and put us on a regular basis, with a monthly allowance for men and officers to be credited against their accounts on the army paybooks."

Colonel Kangleon promoted me to major for the speech. He said it gave him back his army.

But the army was done shooting Filipinos. The Japs finally settled the Miranda problem for us. Miranda had a camp named "Camp Heaven." It was ideally situated for defensive purposes, on hills and with sheer cliffs on three sides. On the night of December 6 a typhoon blew up. Miranda's guards came in out of it, but the Japs didn't. They walked right through it, led by fifth columnists, and into Miranda's camp and smashed the whole works, capturing or killing all but a few of his men. Miranda himself got away. He went into hiding and stayed there until we captured him.

After the battle of Baybay our army's first problem— more immediate even than establishing a civil government and getting paid—was ammunition. They had shot off almost everything they had. Besides, they had been using battery separators and battery terminal lead as well as other soft metals for their bullets. With soft metal like that, you fire a few times and the rifling of the barrel fills up. Then you get a recoil that throws you ten feet.

The whole ordnance problem became my baby. I had made a deal with Colonel McLish, before leaving him, for four thousand empty .30-caliber cartridges. We'd load them and give him back one thousand loaded cartridges in exchange. I found a kid named Kuizon to organize an ordnance factory for us. We scrounged around and got a hand forge, some hacksaws, and a file. That was the small-arms factory.

This boy Kuizon did all the experimenting. He was about twenty-one, the son of a pharmacist from Bato. He had never been in the army before, but I made him a third lieutenant because he was so ingenious and willing.

We foraged in schoolhouses for the bullets to fill the shells. The brass curtain rods there were made of a good hard metal just a little bit thicker than a .30-caliber bullet. We cut the rod up into appropriate lengths, then filed the end down to point it. There was an old broken-down Springfield rifle there, and they'd stick the bullet in this, take a rod, and try to ram it through. If it went, it fit. If it didn't, they'd file some more.

For the primer, we used sulphur mixed with coconut shell carbon. Later we were able to get hold of some antimony and add it to the mixture. Then it worked 80 to 90 per cent efficiently. Our main source of powder was from Japanese sea mines that we would dismantle. We'd mix in pulverized wood to retard the burning because mine powder is too violent a propellant for a rifle bullet. It took us blowing up about five rifles—blowing off the firing pins, the extractors, and the bolts—to find out about that.

All measuring was done rudely, by thumb and by guess and by God. You'd pour the powder into the cartridge with a little homemade funnel sort of thing until you thought you had enough. Then you'd put the piece off the brass curtain rod into the cartridge and crimp the cartridge around it with a pair of pliers. Presto, you had a loaded round. Each bullet had to be tested for fit because all our cartridges had been fired once or twice or four times before. We'd load and extract each round. If the shoulder was too big, we'd crimp it down. If it was too small, we'd say that was fine.

Getting the right measure for the mixture was Kuizon's business.

Springfield 1903

It was all trial and error. When there was an error, the cartridge would rupture in the gun. Hot gases would flash past the bolt and burn his hands. One morning he broke three rifles in succession, burning his hands three times and jolting his shoulder so badly his toes ached.

"Sir, I do not like to do this work, sir," he admitted finally. "I will put the rifle on the table, sir, and test by long distance, sir."

Finally we managed to dragoon an apothecary's scales, and after a few more tests "by long distance" no more rifles blew up. Using this ammunition was hard on our guns, but it worked and killed a Jap to beat hell. The boys liked them because the mine powder gave the bullets so much power they never had to figure windage.

Our ordnance factory never filled more than a one-room house, about twenty feet by ten. But we expanded it to make extractors and firing pins out of such steel as we could find—usually spring steel. These weren't very successful, but they worked fine for a dozen rounds. I put sixty soldiers to work in the ordnance plant, but the filing of the brass curtain rods to fit took so long that our production never got better than an average of 160 bullets a day.

The war had made Filipino politics very simple. There was only one program and one party as far as we were concerned—the "Drive Out the Japs" party. The Japs, on the other hand, were all complicated up in their politics. They were trying to be friendly and get everybody on their side, but they were trying also to get rich off everybody. These are two horses that are very hard to hitch to the same wagon, but the Japs made a try with something they called "The Good Neighbor Association." You be a good neighbor to us and we'll be good to you. You work for us, harvesting copra, selling food, etc., and we will be pals.

The guerrillas replied by killing one "good neighbor" for every guerrilla or guerrilla sympathizer killed. That was the way they played politics in our part of town. Kangleon was much distressed by this, but a guerrilla leader's control over his men is "elastic." He can lead them only where they want to go. I found this out in arguing with Captain Cinco, who had been "unified" by Kangleon.

Cinco (pronounced Sinko) was about thirty years old, with an appearance of being powerfully built. He had been a tartenela (driver of a two-wheeled horse carriage) before the war, then had become a guerrilla leader. He was enjoying himself very much. He had more women than any other man I have ever known. But I have never seen him smile. Filipino faces are usually very expressive. There is a nearly liquid flow to them and their emotions become flasks shaping their faces. Cinco's face appears frozen. His lips hardly move when he talks. In addition, he has mastered—deliberately, I think—the technique of never blinking his eyes, and when he talks to you he looks unblinkingly into your eyes without deviation during the whole length of the conversation. It is very disconcerting. Leading a man like that is a matter of tying a rope around his neck, unless you are leading him where he wants to go.

Cinco's men developed the habit of killing Japan's "good neighbors," leaving their faces untouched so that they might be recognized but mincing up their bodies gruesomely, then floating them downstream to their home barrio where they could serve as an example to the others. If there was no stream, they'd sneak the bodies into the main square at night and leave them there. It was an ugly kind of "politics," but the number of "good neighbors" decreased so radically that the Japs all but stopped executing guerrilla sympathizers for a while.

Where politics were reduced to so elemental a basis, it was not hard to establish a civil government. The Japs had got hold of all but one member of the former provincial board for Leyte. They kept them in their garrison areas, where they were permitted to function under Japanese supervision. In the towns and barrios that the Japs had not garrisoned, municipal mayors or tinentes and officials in general functioned in complete autonomy, visited now and then by Japanese patrols but with decreasing regularity during 1943 as our strength increased and life for Japanese patrols became more hazardous. Each locality had its own police, but in most cases we disarmed them to equip the army, and what they did was patrol around with homemade shotguns or just clubs.

Governor Demiterio, who had presided over Leyte in 1924, was made leader of our government by Kangleon and was installed in the municipal building at Maasin. The regular municipal functionaries were in most cases left untouched. The functions of the government were very limited. There was a loyalty tax to be collected from the people. The rate was originally 10 centavos a month for each male from eighteen to sixty, but I ordered the governor to increase that to 25 centavos a month after getting hold of a *Life* magazine that told of the war effort in America. The people could be sold the idea by the story of the great job being done back home. The tax would be collected by municipal officials whose treasurers would turn it in to our provincial government.

The legal hold Kangleon had over the governor was his power to appoint an army civil administration officer for the region in case he deemed it necessary. The mere existence of this power made it unnecessary ever actually to use it.

The government proved very useful to us. It acted as "the goat" on all guerrilla actions disapproved of by the people. It bore the expense of all improvements mutually beneficial to our army and the population—road repairs, for example, and bridges, a telegraph system that I installed later. Kangleon had an army mind. He didn't care whose money was spent as long as it wasn't the army's. Because of the civil government, I was able to give our army a number of advantages that Kangleon would have regarded as "frills" if they had to be paid for out of his funds.

We were all working against time in those days. We knew that as soon as we became strong enough to worry the Japs, they would move in and crush us. We hoped to have some surprises for them when they moved in. We didn't expect to be able to win until MacArthur returned, but we did count on killing Japs and on keeping alive in the people the hope of eventual liberation.

18

The new government's "Proclamation No. 1" was drawn up by me. It precipitated the first of a number of quarrels that I had with Kangleon, resulting in a final rupture between us.

The proclamation stipulated that on or before September 25, 1943, the following materials necessary to the prosecution of the war must be delivered by whoever owned them to the nearest municipal mayor. There were listed paper, tires, lubricating oils, greases, firearms, ammunition, gunpowders, various chemicals needed by ordnance, files, saws, hammers, batteries, radios, motors and engines, gunny sacks for a uniform for our soldiers, paints, nails—all the way down to thread, buttons, and screws.

I knew Kangleon would object to confiscation of these materials without payment, but I prepared for that. I remembered a civilian whose automobile had been confiscated by Colonel Cornell near Tacloban before the surrender and made a rather hazardous journey to find out what form of payment he had received. He showed me a U. S. Army voucher receipt and contract of sale. I copied the form and put into the proclamation that we would pay by voucher.

"Those failing to respond voluntarily to this appeal are subject to confiscation without payment as withholding war material."

This provision was satisfactory to the colonel, but what we jumped down each other's throats about was this: an informant providing information to the military authorities about withheld material would receive as his reward 20 per cent in cash or kind of the material confiscated; all houses, upon receipt of proper information, were to be subject to search by the military.

It didn't look pretty to the colonel. He thought it would alienate the people and divide them among themselves and make for a kind of country he wouldn't care to live in. It didn't look pretty to me either, but I had never heard of a pretty war and I felt we had to be practical. The colonel hardly had paper to write his dispatches to subordinates. How was the government going to print money for us, I demanded of Kangleon, if we couldn't give it the paper, the ink, and the dies?

"The people must offer what they have voluntarily, out of love for liberation."

"How are they going to feel love for liberation if we have no propaganda department, if we have no radio to get news, if we have no paper to write news on, no ink, no cars, no tires to distribute news?"

I won finally. The clause went in, but both Kangleon and myself had been wrong. The clause did not alienate people. It did not set one against the other. The people remained about as ever. They simply ignored the clause and its opportunity for a 20 per cent unearned increment. There never was a single case of a neighbor telling on another.

However, the proclamation worked fine in every other respect. We got great masses of stuff—mostly junk, but usable with a little patching and renovation. Then we added to it by raiding Chinese shops. The Chinese of the Philippines were in considerable part representative of old China in their thinking—the China that was not a nation but a grab bag for war lords. To them all governments were alien and all causes treacherous. They lived their separate lives in the Filipino communities, untouched by any nationalistic upsurge, the various tides of war meaning to them only a change in the faces of masters with whom they intended to co-operate only as far as necessary. The Chinese made only token offerings of their goods for our vouchers. The Filipinos did not inform on the Chinese, but we knew they had more than they had offered us so we raided them and made a considerable haul wherever we struck. The raids created no antagonisms among the people, not even among the Chinese. They accepted it as part of the game.

We got two thousand gunny sacks from the raids, and Kangleon designed a uniform that could be made from them. It consisted of a short-sleeved shirt and short or long trousers, depending on the preferences of the men. We got seven hundred uniforms out of the two thousand sacks. They were harsh to the skin; but uniform and warm.

The mint ran out of paper to make money before the proclamation was issued. My idea was to have the army print its own money, but Quezon refused. He said that must remain the province of the civil government. I imagine he figured it would be too easy for an army to balance its books. The proclamation put the mint back in business.

A jeweler, who did engraving on the side, made wood blocks for us. I had some of Fertig's Mindanao money as a model, but Kangleon insisted on adding pictures to it—a carabao, a nipa hut, local scenery. It looked nearly official by the time we finished.

We started off on 20-centavo bills—paper dimes. The mint worked on an assembly-line basis in an old schoolhouse. One man would cut the paper to size, another would place it in a frame, stamp the wood block into a pad of ink, then press it onto the paper. The ink had to dry before the paper could be turned over to be printed on the reverse side. It took a long time.

I am no good at cost accounting, but after a week I began to get worried. There were nine men there and in a week they had not printed up enough money to pay themselves their own salaries. I made a rough stab at working out the expenses and found out it was costing us 40 centavos to print one 20-centavo bill. After that, we had new blocks made and stuck to 20-peso bills, where each bill represented a profit of 19 pesos and 60 centavos—$9.80. We had been authorized to issue 2,500,000 pesos.

We did not worry about counterfeiters. We had all the paper there was. We used all kinds. We'd have used toilet paper if we could have got it. Some of our money was printed on wrapping paper, some on Grade 3 note-book paper, lined and all. We ran out of dye pretty fast. That was the fault of the women. The women there made their own clothing out of abacá fiber—a rope-colored Manila hemp. They couldn't stand looking all alike, so we were out of dyes. In the end we made our own ink by taking a crude oil lamp, putting a hood over it, and trapping the soot. We mixed the soot with glycerin and printed news sheets as well as money with it.

19

As chief of staff, I naturally felt it necessary to have a staff to be chief of. When I came into the picture the colonel and his eldest son, Loloy, were all the staff there was. There was no G1, G2, G3, G4, no signals officer, no judge advocate general to handle court-martial cases, no psychological warfare department, no medical corps, no paymaster, no transportation corps.

I found people to head up all these branches—Frederico Coaeyes, former pilot who knew regulations and knew people, he was G1; Dr. Posoncuoy, a Spanish mestizo boy, was the best G2 you can imagine until June, 1944, when he was killed by the Japs; G3, our operations, was headed by Capt. Joe Nazareno, a fine guerrilla fighter who had led the wiping out of two Japanese launches and had had a number of engagements with Jap patrols; G4 was Gordon Lang, an American who had been yeoman second class in the navy, stationed at Cebu.

Gordon had sat around Leyte for seven or eight months very quietly until the Japs began pressing him too hard. Then he got ten or twelve Filipinos together and wiped out the next patrol that came bothering him. He submitted to unification with Colonel Kangleon very readily.

Propaganda was run by Gorden Veloso, a former politician. We gave him a radio as his news source, and he turned the news into fiery words which were distributed by our transportation corps. Gordon Lang—who started as a typical American "souvenir hunter" and turned that yearning into the source material for a greater quartermaster—started our transportation corps by contributing a motorcycle he had got from Teting Escano. We added a station wagon that somebody—we never did find out who—had hidden in the jungle from the Japs. It was a brand-new Ford V-8. We got from civilians and paid for by voucher a Ford truck, an International and a Chevrolet, two Ford V-8 sedans and one Buick sedan. We could not spare paint to make them look like army cars. One truck had "International Coconut Corporation" painted all over it. We let it stay.

Gasoline was a nearly immediate problem. The Japs had taken all they could find. But Frank Laird got us over this hurdle. He was an American about forty-five who had served fifteen years in the army and then had been discharged because of his heart. "You learn how to do anything in the army," he said, and we got him some barrels, galvanized pipe, elbows, and a wrench or two, and he went into the petrol business, distilling alcohol out of tuba. He managed to get a 90-per cent alcohol concentration out of the tuba, and we called Laird Chief Distillery Officer.

The cars would run on the alcohol all right if you opened up the gasoline jets on the carburetors or reamed them out to let in more alcohol than they would gasoline. There wasn't much power to the stuff—unless you drank it—but the cars ran and they made six to eight miles on a gallon. The boys took to sipping the fuel, but they stopped that when one of them went blind temporarily. Laird was using galvanized pipe in the distilleries. For a drinking still, you have to have copper tubing. We got around to that later when things were well organized, using the copper tubing off the gas lines of wrecked automobiles.

The fuel was rather treacherous. It absorbed water very quickly. If you left half a bottle around with the cork off, in a few hours it would fill right up to the top, the tuba alcohol soaking up moisture right out of the air. The water would give our cars all kinds of trouble. But we finally had the tuba growers organized—paying them 50 centavos for a five-gallon can of the unfermented palm juice—and had seven plants running all day long and a separate still to make drinking fuel. The rainy season knocked our production down considerably by lowering the alcohol yield from the tuba. But our production on the main plant at Maasin kept fairly consistently to a daily average of from five to six gallons.

The drinking liquor we got, being strong enough to run a car on, was also strong enough not to taste so good. Then Laird discovered that the addition of glycerin, oil of peppermint, green vegetable coloring matter, and a little sugar syrup made something good enough to call crème de menthe. The great advantage it had was we could make it and drink it in the same day. The advantage was so overpowering it nearly overpowered the mint. The mint needed the glycerin to make ink.

I took the signal corps under my special supervision. I wanted communications so that, wherever our radio station was, reports could come into it quickly. Kangleon had been getting along with runners who would take anywhere from a week to a month or two to make their round trips. He didn't want to be "fancy." He was afraid a working communications setup would make the Japs think we were stronger than we were, and they would hit us before we were ready to put up a show. But when I pointed out the civil government could be prevailed upon to defray the expenses and the funds would not have to come from the army, Kangleon decided to risk it and gave me the go-ahead. It was a legitimate expenditure for the civil government. It and the population would be allowed to use the system, too.

The population had cut down all the telephone wires soon after the Japs came in. It was a patriotic move, and also the wire could be shaped into nails for making bancas and houses. Nails were scarcer in southern Leyte at the time than new gold teeth. So wire was our first shortage. I got a supply by sending the army out to take the barbed wire off all the fences in our area. Then I put soldiers to work with pliers, taking the barbs off—hammered out, they made fine small nails—unwinding the wire, stretching it, and rolling it on spools.

For insulators, I called on an old bodega and accumulated a supply of old soda pop bottles. Where we could find telegraph poles, we wired the bottles to the top of them. But mostly we constructed our communications on palm trees. The telegraph poles in southern Leyte had been made of termite- and bug- and python- and bird- and tornado-proof pipe—too useful in fish traps and as house beams for the people to let alone.

In a month and a half we were able to put up approximately 140 kilometers of telegraph lines.

Our wet-cell batteries required the addition of copper sulphate crystals rather than acid. We raided every old telegraph station in the district to get these and whatever other equipment was around, keys, relays, and so forth, but for the life of the system they always had to be rationed on a priority basis.

Governor Demiterio at our request provided us with the telegraph operators. He called all former operators back to active duty at their old salaries—30 to 70 pesos a month. If they hadn't come, the army would have got after them. But they were all glad to come. They had been unemployed ever since the Japs had arrived.

Almost the first messages I sent out were general orders to all unit commanders: (1) no regular enrolled member of the guerrilla army would be regarded as a deserter by either the Filipino Army or the United States Army; (2) all guerrilla army men who had served previous to September 1, 1943, would be paid from the time of the surrender to date of termination of their services; (3) all men enlisting after September 1 would be paid from the date of enlistment, regardless of previous service in the regular army; (4) monthly allowance against full pay— which could not be paid over at once but must be carried on the books until victory—herewith increased from 19 to 24 pesos a month; (5) a pious hope that the substantial sum of money to be paid each man after victory as salary due would be spent wisely for a farm or to start a small business.

Well, then we had the makings of an army. We had communications twenty-four hours a day. It expedited intelligence reports enormously. Intelligence was the primary mission of each unit in a Jap garrison area. Kangleon wanted to know every time a Jap sneezed, and now the telegraph told him the same day the Jap sneezed, not a week or two months later. We had uniforms. I got a monthly roster of officers and troops. The pay allowances were checked very thoroughly. We had to imbue the troops with a feeling of confidence on that because, after all, everything we were doing was based on wind, that's all, just hope, and hope needs faith, belief, confidence. The men were being drilled and taken through practice exercises in ambushes, night maneuvers, forced marches, and target practice—without bullets, we could not spare the bullets, but they practiced rifle holding, trigger squeezing, windage, elevation, and estimation of distances by triangulation.

Companies were organized on a regular army basis—with a guardhouse, barracks, mess hall, officers' quarters. These structures might be any houses or huts they found around in the hills. There would be regular guard mount, and there was even such a thing as being AWOL. The men were continually asking time off to help their wives when they expected a baby, or at planting time or harvest time or after a typhoon when the roof back home had blown off. They'd ask for six days and get three and take two weeks. The officer could then use the guardhouse or his fists. Most of our officers used their fists.

The guerrilla army was supported by the population. Under urging by the provincial government a whole network of volunteer guards sprang up—civilians serving without pay, donating one day out of every four to act as sentinels or relay men for messages or lookouts. When Japanese approached, the civilians were warned, too, and in the hills and many coastal barrios enemy patrols found only empty houses and vacant towns—not even a dog to them, the dogs having buqweed off with their owners.

And we had a medical corps. I made Doc Parado our chief surgeon because he had been such a good fighter. I then enrolled all civilian doctors and dentists in a reserve and concentrated all medicines and all medical instruments in the area in one place. In that way we had a genuinely mobile hospital unit. All the instruments filled only two ordinary doctors' satchels. The hospital was any home we found around.

Maybe it wasn't a New York Medical Center, but it certainly was mobile.

20

In the meantime, I was seeing Curly. Tom Jurika had told me she was at the Casa in Malitbog. He had come up to get in on our guerrilla movement.

"Congratulations," he said.

"What for?"

"Why, don't you know? They're all prepared to kill the fatted calf up there for you, my prodigal son. The wedding can take place any time now."

"Whose wedding? To who?"

"Didn't you tell Don Lorenzo you felt like settling down in the Philippines, buy ten thousand coconut trees, and live the life of plenty?"

"Yes, but I didn't ask to marry him. He's married already."

"That's what sold him. Then he knew you were sincere."

"Sincere about what? Hell, that was just cigar smoke coming out of my mouth, the ten thousand coconut trees, after a good chow. Sincere about who?"

"But, didn't you send for Curly? Didn't you write a letter to tell her to come to see you?"

"To come see her cousins, and I'd be in the neighborhood."

"Well, if you ask a girl to come see you, it's an old Spanish custom to take that as meaning your intentions are honorable."

"Gosh, what do you know about that?"

"I think you're lucky. Now there will be a two- or three-week phase where you'll be a very agreeable house guest. After that, there will be a sort of 'Young man, what

132

are your intentions?' Then you'll have to either stay or go."

"But for Christ sake . . ."

"Why do you think a girl like that would come over to see you if it wasn't for marriage?"

"But gee, for Christ sake, Tom, it was to see her cousins, not me."

"I knew a fellow once," said Tom, "who went calling on his girl only to see his prospective mother-in-law. But he was a dope. Curly's no dope."

That seemed to me for a day or two to put a big, wet, sticky blanket over the whole thing. I didn't want to get married. I didn't want to live in the Philippines. The Philippines were just a platform to me on which to have an argument with the Japs. But the temptation was too great, and four days after I returned I asked Kangleon for leave and he gave me two and one-half days.

The whole family stood on the big main stairway of the Casa, waiting to greet me. Don Lorenzo, the head of the household, was there and his wife and Enday, his daughter, Nonita, who was Don Lorenzo's other daughter, Nonita's husband Ed who was Curly's brother, Teting and Loling, and Curly.

Gee, she looked beautiful! I mean Curly. I hadn't seen her in more than a year, but she was more beautiful even than I had remembered her. I hadn't intended to kiss her. I had intended to be very offhand there and friendly, with, you know, one of those friend-of-the-family, how's everything-with-you,-dear manners, but she looked so beautiful. She had a silk housecoat on, extending clear to the floor. It's just like a dress, but girls call it a housecoat. It was gray silk, almost white, and had thin blue designs in it, sort of like a Chinese design but mostly white silk. Gosh, she looked just beautiful and the sight of her . . . well, I walked up those stairs like I was lifted and I didn't see anybody but her. The other people were just sort of things standing around there, and I dropped my pack and stood looking at her like she was General MacArthur coming on a battleship.

"Well, if you kissed me good-by," I said, "we ought to kiss hello."

Then I remembered what Tom had said and the kiss didn't turn out to be anything to write home about, just a short, hasty sort of a peck thing. When I looked around, there the whole family was standing beaming approval.

I took occasion at dinner to tell the family that submarines were going to come in to bring supplies and take out the Americans who had been ordered out. Curly's face fell. My heart fell, too, but I stuck to it and that night I didn't even kiss her good night. I just said, "Good night, Curly."

The next night, Johnny Escano started to work on the piano and, after the rest of the family went to bed, Curly and I started to work on some punch they had made— Hacienderos. *Hacienda* is Spanish for house and they gave the drink that name because it is a kind of planter's punch arrangement. It's the punch of a mule, a white one. Johnny is a good guy and a marvelous pianist. He plays the guitar, too. He studied in America in Boulder, Colorado, and he can play anything anybody could think of from Bach to "Honky-Tonk Train Blues." We all drank punch and he played and we sang and it was very nice there. It was like home when home is full of nice people whom you like very much.

Curly said the punch had made her feel a little sick. She went out on the veranda and I went with her. Johnny kept working the piano. He played sad and low and to his heart. He wouldn't let go of the piano. He had it really talking to him. In the patio below the veranda there were big quiet dark blue trees, spreading out and down towards the bay. The moon was low. We could see it on the bay, a cold glitter there, like something in a cellophane box, a box of glitter, and the moonlight came through the branches of the dark blue trees. It seemed to be lace then, the white way it came through there, and blowy way, and with designs in it from the shadows. I told this to Curly. I pointed the moonlight out to her. She didn't say anything. She was feeling pretty sick from the punch. The big quiet white Casa with its windows like dark eyes shining stood behind us and out of it came the sound of Johnny at the piano, making the piano talk low to his heart.

She looked so darn funny and beautiful as she stood being sick in the moonlight. I put my arm around her and led her to the balustrade.

"Okay," I said, "up we go."

She couldn't do it. She tried, but couldn't. So I put my finger down her throat. Then it came.

"It's awful, but I feel better."

Oh hell, this sounds so bad. It sounds so crumby, but that's the way it happened and I loved her from then on. She just sood there sort of weaving with a funny grin on her face, looking uneasy and trying not to show how uneasy she felt. Johnny had gone upstairs by then. There was nobody awake any more. I got Curly some water. I couldn't find a glass, only a big white pitcher. I held it to her lips and the water spilled down both sides of her face. We both laughed at that. We laughed into each other's faces. It seemed the funniest thing that had ever happened to anybody. She looked so cute laughing that I put the pitcher down and kissed her. It was no short hasty peck sort of thing either.

"The war is tough," I told Curly.

"What means that—tough?"

"It means," I said, "that I don't know from one minute to the next where I'll be and that I have to go where I'm ordered and do what I'm ordered."

"The Japs cannot live forever."

"We can't either."

"The Japs cannot live so long as us. Not here. Not in my islands."

"Do you know what we are here?" I told Curly. "We are a tick in their hide. All the building we do, all the work, all the planning, all the hoping, all the effort there that we put in, it is just to build ourselves up to be a tick in their hide. Then the minute they feel the itch of us, they reach with their two fingers and squash."

"You be the tick. I'll be the tock. Then we are tick-tock together."

She had such an expressive face. She was not like the American girls. Everything she felt came out on her face. I could look at her face for hours at a time. It was like listening to music or to a conversation that you wanted to

135

hear. When she said "together," you could see the meaning of the word on her face.

When I got back, I told Kangleon we ought to move the headquarters. We were installed then at Maasin in the big concrete schoolhouse next to the municipal building where the provincial government sat. I wanted him to go to Sogod, which would be nearer Malitbog. I didn't want him to go to Malitbog because I was afraid Don Lorenzo would move out. He always entertained all Americans and guerrillas who came there. He made a point of it. If the headquarters moved, he'd insist on the staff taking his house. Then there might not be room for him.

"This is a good place," Kangleon said. "I like it here."

"Sogod would be better."

"No, no, my boy. Maasin is fine. I like it."

Then, one fine morning a four-engined Jap bomber came right smack over the schoolhouse at a distance of about three hundred feet. We could see the Jap crew waving down at us. They knew exactly where we were and what we were dong. We stood stupefied. The guard out front just stood leaning on his rifle looking at the plane. Two days later, a two-engine plane came over very low.

"I think we'll move to Malitbog," the colonel said.

"Sogod is better. It is more central for us."

"Malitbog has Don Lorenzo's Casa."

"I don't think Malitbog is a very good idea, Colonel. Yes sir, I don't. Sogod is better."

But the colonel had decided on Malitbog, and Don Lorenzo with his usual hospitality and loyalty to our cause promptly turned the Casa over to us and moved out. However, Curly remained, and the boys and their wives and Cap and Mrs. Martin. So it worked out fine.

I lived at the Casa until October 27. Then a message came from Colonel Fertig, summoning us to his headquarters before November 1. We thought it meant evacuation to Australia for me as well as for the others.

We had a fine big launch for the trip. Captain Valley had captured it.

The launch was seagoing. It had come in with fifteen

Japs, probably direct from Japan itself. They were a naval party, to judge by the insignia. They had come ashore to get coconuts and see if they could find some meat. Valley's men had surrounded them, carrying their rifles slung across the backs of their necks with bunches of coconuts hanging from the stocks and from the barrels. They ringed the Japs around unostentatiously. Then, when they had got in close, they had dropped the coconuts and opened fire. They killed seven on the beach. One got away into the jungle. Five were killed in the water, wading and swimming back to the launch. One was killed on the launch. His body hung over the rail.

That left one. He remained hiding on the boat for three days and three nights. He didn't dare show himself to cast off the lines. But they knew he was there because every time they shouted out an offer to him to surrender they'd have to move fast. He fired at the sound of their voices.

On the fourth morning they made like an attack from the shore on the starboard side of the launch. While he was banging away at that, one of the men boarded the launch from the port side and killed him.

So then we had a navy as well as an army.

21

My primary mission on Leyte was not as a major and chief of staff, but as ensign in the United States Navy assigned to construct a radio network to spy on Jap shipping. But it seemed to me that we could not count on the radio network functioning unless we had a guerrilla army to back it up. That's why I spent so much time with Kangleon, building the network from the ground up.

We already had one station manned by an American—Truman Heminway, a Vermont boy. I brought back with me from my first trip to Fertig two men to train as radio operators. One was Joseph St. John, who had been with me on the banca in which we had tried to make Australia. He was the real thing. He worked conscientiously all the way through. The other boy got himself into a jam in a little while. He got caught in a fight with the Japs and killed some and came jazzing back to town feeling he wanted a girl. He wanted a girl right away. He went into a Chinese store and asked the old Chinaman there where he could find a girl. The Chinaman stuttered around a bit. An argument started and the upshot of it was this boy shot the Chinaman and killed him. Kangleon turned the business over to the civil government to handle. They gave the boy four years in jail.

I put an army man named Chapman—a boy from Los Angeles—in charge of the station we already had and left St. John there for training and asked Heminway to take an old Bureau of Posts radio that we had found and set it up in Samar overlooking San Bernardino Straits. Heminway was willing. He had a wife, Kitty, and he said he was going to name the station after her. She went along with him.

The Bureau of Posts radio was one hundred miles from where we were. It took Heminway about three weeks to get to it, and another week for him to get it running. It came on the air powerfully, the most powerful set on the islands. It worked for about two minutes. Then the transformer started to smoke.

Heminway broke out of code and into voice. "Hold the line, Bub," he said. "I am burning up."

"Pour some cold water on yourself," St. John told him.

"Call me back later when this thing cools off."

The transformer never did work for longer than two minutes at a time. Then it would start to smoke.

Coming in to the beach by Fertig's headquarters we nearly got our heads blown off. All they saw was a Jap launch. But we had an American flag and waved it like crazy and finally they stopped shooting.

Then Chick Parsons jumped on me with both feet about the radio setup.

"You're in the doghouse as far as the navy is concerned," he said.

"Look," I said, "there was an army to get going."

"All right, so what's that?"

"We've got a lot of soldiers, that's what it is, and we've got them in an army."

"So you've got a lot of soldiers and you've got guns and you kill a Jap now and then or a dozen or a hundred. Okay, you did a good job, boy. But you are in the navy. MacArthur doesn't care if you never kill a Jap. He wants intelligence out of you. He's got a one-track mind when it comes to intelligence."

"Well, Christ almighty! I don't get this. We're ordered to unify so that we can get aid, so that we can get radio sets. It seems to me we are attacking the problem from the same angle. How can we have a radio setup unless we can unify and get radios. How can we keep it going unless we have an army to give it some kind of protection—warning at least that the Japs are on the way?"

"Look, my boy," said Parsons. "This is definite. You are needed on intelligence."

It griped the hell out of me, but I said, "Okay, we'll get this squared around."

However, the big news around there was that a submarine was coming in with supplies and to take out Americans. It was like a regular convention around there. Fertig had called in about five hundred soldiers to help with the unloading. He had summoned all the guerrilla

leaders from as far away as Manila, ostensibly to coordinate their activities but actually, too, so that they might see the submarine and the aid America was giving. Then he had got together two truckloads of fresh vegetables and fruits—onions, tomatoes, pineapples, those remarkable Filipino bananas a taste of which makes the bananas we get in America seem inedible, guabane, coconuts, fresh beans—to give to the submarine. He wanted them to bring back word to Souwespac that he had a real organization going.

So secret is the silent service that only Fertig knew when the submarine was coming in. At the last minute, he tipped us off and we all walked over to a little bay about six miles from the headquarters. There was a beautiful dock there. Our army had tried to blow it up before the surrender, but fortunately for us had failed. Then, about four-thirty in the afternoon, a cry went up all along the beach. A submarine was surfacing.*

We had two launches out there to guide her in. I was in charge of one of them. The 10th Division orchestra, dressed up in white shirts and white pants, played "Aloha" and "Anchors Aweigh" and "Aloha" again and "The Stars and Stripes Forever."

"Where in the hell are we?" yelled a sailor from the deck of the sub.

There were seven trucks waiting on the pier and a big lighter was waiting out in the water and there were small, medium, and large bancas bobbing all over.

"It looks like we made a wrong turn," said another sailor, "and wound up in Hollywood."

The channel was very narrow for the submarine, but they handled her beautifully. It was a classic example of ship handling. I was very proud of the navy that day in front of all those Filipinos. The vessel just greased up to the dock with no trouble at all, no pain and no strain.

She looked as big as a battleship to us. She was carrying tommy guns, carbines, hand grenades, bazookas, 20-millimeter cannons, mounts off old PT boats, .50-caliber machine guns with tripod mounts and ammunition in belts, ammunition for all the guns, jungle camouflage suits, regular GI suntans, jungle boots, insignia, cigarettes, chocolate, Spam, cheese, the chocolate out of K rations, magazines, books, MacArthur's *I Shall Return* magazine, as we

---

*For the thrilling story of supplying our irregular troops in the Philippines, read *GUERRILLA SUBMARINES,* another volume in the Bantam War Book Series.

called it, although it calls itself *Free Philippines*. It is a picture publication, on the style of *Life*. All the cigarettes, chocolates, and food had "I shall return—MacArthur" wrappers around them.

Being a naval officer, I made a beeline for the wardroom. The captain made me feel at home over a cup of

Tommy Gun

coffee. I drank nine cups one after the other. I had a hand of native tobacco with me, very strong, and after finishing the coffee I proceeded to roll myself a cigar.

"Would you like to try one?" I asked.

The engineering officer was the first to bite. He took one puff and put it down hastily. "Off the skin of what dead animals do they scrape this?" he asked. Then he suggested I try one of his—which was what I had wanted in the first place. I smoked cigarettes chain fashion all the time I was on board. I couldn't get enough of them.

I contributed my hand of native tobacco to the ship's small stores.

"Really," they said, "your kindness is overwhelming."

But I also gave them some Jap souvenirs. They were glad to get those.

"Oh boy," said one of the kids to whom I gave a pack of Jap cigarettes, "wait till I tell Ruthie how I swam aboard a torpedoed Jap battleship singlehanded to get these for her."

The boys cut me in on the news from the outside world. I remember how startled I was to hear that Kaiser was building Liberty ships in six days.

"Now, I'll tell one," I said.

No, they said, there was a boy there who had been in San Francisco four months before and he had the cold dope.

Holy cow! San Francisco! Four months ago!

Those boys gave me everything I could carry off the ship. They gave me sixteen cartons of cigarettes and pipe tobacco, and the skipper gave me his new twelve-dollar Kirsten pipe. "Hell," he said, "I'll be back in Pearl in another three, four months. I can get all I want there."

I asked him what he wanted most out of the Philippines, I would get it for him. He asked for ebony. He liked to sculpt in wood. I never saw the skipper again, but the ebony—the most beautiful piece I could find—is hidden on Leyte, and after the war, if he is still alive and I am, I am going to get it to him. The ebony is safe.

They gave me all the cherry pie I could get down, genuine cherry pie with cherries that you could taste the North American climate in, and big thick cheese sandwiches, and a razor and razor blades, soap, hair oil, shaving cream—all the stuff that when you dream about it you wake up with a smile on your face. They gave me books, too. They said they really couldn't give me any, they were navy property, but if I picked out the ones I wanted and dropped them over the side, then they could say they had lost them over the side. I picked out a collection of Winston Churchill's speeches, a thick volume of American short stories, a volume of digested Pacific articles, *They Call It Pacific* by Clark Lee, and your book, *Battle for the Solomons,* and Carlos Romulo's book and Christopher Morley's *Kitty Foyle* for Curly.

Then Fertig came on board with the guerrilla leaders, including Kangleon. They had never been aboard a naval vessel before. You can imagine the awe on their faces when they saw the splendor and power, the stainless steel interiors, the smooth engines purring in their oil like cats in cream.

Kangleon put in a bid for supplies for his force right away. "Shotguns and shotgun shells," he said. "It's the best thing for blowing Japs out of the underbrush."

"All right, if you want them," Parsons told him, "but a case of shotgun shells takes up the same space as twelve thousand rounds of carbine ammunition."

"Twelve thousand rounds?"

"Yes, on a submarine it's space that counts, not weight."

"Then I want the carbine ammunition. Whatever is most."

"But twelve thousand rounds of carbine ammunition takes up the same space as sixty carbines."

"But I want carbines, too, and tommy guns, a lot of them."

"How about dental equipment? Haven't you got any teeth left there in your army?"

"Medicines! Medicines, too. Ten kits. How much space do they take?"

I tell you all this to show you how much there is to know before you can operate on a shoestring. Enthusiasm, patriotism, guts, ingenuity, they are all fine things, but they only get you six feet under unless there is knowledge to go with them. Parsons had it. He knew navy.

Everything was so well organized by Fertig that we got the submarine unloaded and away, with about thirty Americans on it, by midnight. Tom Jurika was on board. He hated to go. He had had one close shave, but he wanted more. He had become absorbed in the fight.

M1 Carbine

He had been out on an errand with Gordon Smith and Joe Escano, whom I had got into the army as a first lieutenant. We always checked before landing anywhere, and they pulled up alongside a fisherman to ask if any Japs had come into the barrio there.

"Oh, very few only, sir."

Joe picked up his Garand and pointed it at the fisherman. "What do you mean, you son of a bitch! Speak up, boy!"

"Only a hundred, sir," replied the fisherman.

Tom and Gordon got down in the bottom of the

banca. "I see one," said Joe, "no, there are two. By God, there are more coming. They are walking down to the beach and looking at us."

"Well, Joe, darling," said Tom, "what the hell are we waiting for?"

It was a sweaty time. Wind and current were against them. Joe had to scull all by himself. He looked more like a Filipino. But when Tom got down to Fertig's and they told him he had to leave, he sent a message to Souwespac:

"Have no desire to leave. Repeat no desire to leave, please."

A dispatch came back: "You will proceed out under orders from General MacArthur."

Tom was a fine quartermaster. They needed someone down there who was acquainted with our supply problems.

When the submarine finally put out, I felt all mixed up. They were going to be in Australia in a little while, in less time than it would take me to get back to Leyte. If I had gone, I could be back in the navy. I could be talking United States. I was hungry for my own kind. I could be fighting Japs with first-class, made in U.S.A. power, not with soda pop bottles hung up on palm trees by retired barbed wire.

But Curly was in Leyte. That's what mixed me up. If it hadn't been for that, I'd have been crying that midnight when the sub pulled out.

22

Among those present at the submarine was Long Tom Baxter. He had come up a crowded road since shoehorning his way out of jail. After parting with old Dutch and Gordon Smith, he had fallen in with Capt. Khalil Coder—the mighty Coder of the River, as he was called—and Captain Zapanta and they were sitting over some tuba with Mrs. Zapanta when a volunteer guard brought the news a Jap patrol was monkeying around in the neighborhood. The place where they were was well hidden. It was the only good hiding place for miles. It was flat country there, mostly rice paddies. So nobody made a move except Mrs. Zapanta.

"We attack," she said.

The men glanced at each other nervously. They knew her well.

"No, my sweet," said her husband. "Today it is too warm. In the evening perhaps, if the moon is not too early."

It was not country for a hit-and-run attack. It was very good for the hit, but for the run it was worthless.

"All right, you come in the evening, reinforce me." Mrs. Zapanta took up her husband's gun. "I attack now."

"Sweet, my sweet, my very sweetest, you will kill us to force us this way."

"I attack now."

"But, my sweet!"

"There are Japs now. I attack now."

Zapanta looked at the mighty Coder of the River. Then he looked at Long. He seemed very uncomfortable.

"Zapanta, my friend," Long said, "you certainly married a lulu."

"What means that?"

"It means your missus is a lulu."

"If I go where she forces," Zapanta said, "there is a chance I will be killed. If I do not, it is certain. She will attend to it."

"It is clear, Zapanta, you will die of love."

They decided finally to leave Mrs. Zapanta home. She could not run fast enough. The running would be very important in this attack. It was agreed that, to expedite the running, the soldiers with tommy guns—Thompson tommy guns, the Filipino officers called them, seeking to be formal—and with automatic rifles would throw them into a carabao wallow from which they could be retrieved later. A carabao is like a pig and cannot sweat. He needs to lie in mud twice a day. There was a good deep wallow hidden in a declivity along the line of retreat that would hide the heavy guns very well. Long said he would cover the retreat past the wallow with his Garand.

The country did not permit an ambush. There was only grass and rice paddies and an occasional tree. The guerrillas hit. They held their ground a few moments while the Japs deployed. Then the mortars and machine guns started and the guerrillas began to run. Long stood behind a tree. He fired at every Jap who showed his head. He fired wherever sounds of firing were coming from and between times he fired at the spaces in between.

There was one young guerrilla who ran too excitedly to think well.

Garand

148

When he came to the wallow, instead of throwing only his gun in, he threw himself in as well. He climbed out swiftly. Then he ran swiftly. He had got about forty yards when he realized he was still carrying his gun. He ran all the way back into the bullets, threw in his gun, and turned and fled.

Long watched him admiringly. He has everything but brains, he thought.

After that, there were more little things for Long. He found a hand grenade and took up a position near a footbridge over a canyon. The canyon was almost one hundred feet deep. Jap patrols had by that time become very wary of bridges. The first Jap materialized suddenly. He had crawled on his belly to one end of the bridge. Then he had popped up and dashed across and flung himself down in the jungle on Long's side of the canyon.

Long had not intended to waste his grenade on the first. He knew if the first Jap made it, the others would become less wary. A grenade was a great rarity. It could not be employed merely on one. Long did not worry about the Jap on his side of the canyon. Since he had got his Garand one Jap anywhere did not worry him.

Then three Japs came towards the bridge. They did not crawl. They were merely crouched over. Long took the pin out of the grenade. He held it in his hand. A thousand and one, he counted, a thousand and two, a thousand and three, a thousand and four. Then he threw it as high into the air as he could over the bridge. He wanted an air burst that would kill all three Japs at once, or at least blow them off the bridge.

The grenade went in a high arc. It fell steeply. It passed the bridge without exploding and fell into the canyon and lay there silently. Long stood looking down at it disappointedly. Then boom, it went off, reverberating massively in the canyon. It must have had a ten-second fuse.

All the Japs ran frantically to the other side of the canyon, and the patrol withdrew.

Then the guerrillas all got together and decided on something big. They were going to take a town. They picked one that was fat with supplies yet did not have too much garrison, and they moved on it in three columns. Clyde Childress led one. Bill Knortz led the second, and Long led the third.

Knortz was one of the great men of the guerrillas. He had been a college and professional football player back home. Then he had joined the air corps. He studied judo at Hickam Field and won the black belt there. The black belt is as high as you can go in judo. The white belt is first, the brown belt is second, and then the black belt. The only way to win it is to take it off somebody who has it. I think there are only twenty of them in the world. Knortz was a big, immensely powerful, very friendly man. He always carried a BAR with two belts of ammunition—150 rounds—and two .45-caliber pistols. The guns were his undoing. Some months ago, when his banca overturned in a storm, he drowned trying to swim with them. He let go of them too late, when he was too exhausted to go much farther.

There was even a cannon for the attack on the town. It had been made by Captain Zapanta and his wife. The barrell was a piece of gas pipe, three inches in diameter. It was kept from blowing up by metal sleeves and rings. Metal wedges were hammered between the sleeves and the rings to reinforce the barrel further. The firing pin was a tapered marlinespike given tension by rubber bands made from an inner tube. The Zapantas had made three shells for their cannon from three-inch brass pipe filled with battery lead and babbitt, and junk they found around. On to the back of each they had welded a disk. The powder charge was in a case about four inches long. They filled it nearly to the brim with black powder. They wanted to make sure the shell would go. The primer was out of three shotgun shells. Mrs. Zapanta herself had done the ticklish job of forcing the three shotgun primers together and securing them into the back of the shell with sticks of wood so that the marlinespike would hit all three at once. The whole contraption was mounted on wooden wheels. The lanyard was about thirty feet long. They were pretty sure that, if the thing worked at all, there was going to be a recoil.

Where Long's column came into the town, there was

an outpost and supply bodega. He started with about one hundred men. By the time he got within firing distance, there were only twenty left. The rest had faded back, getting a good head start on the retreat they expected to have to make. Long used a kind of roving-center plan of attack. He split his twenty men into two groups of ten. They'd throw a concentrated fire into the outpost from one point, then run quickly to another point and throw concentrated fire from there. The Japs felt outnumbered and retreated into the town.

The supply bodega was full of shoes and *maong*—a kind of dungaree material. When Long started to empty it, he found his column had grown from twenty to three or four hundred. Not only had all his own soldiers returned, but the men of the neighborhood were there, too, helping themselves. The civilians were hard to tell from soldiers. Everybody everywhere was dressed in whatever he could find.

Long was trying to weed out the ringers when a commotion broke out near by. The Japs had left a sniper behind in a tree. Some men had surrounded the tree and ordered the sniper down. He came down quickly. He was a sturdy little boy about ten years old with long, thick, dry black hair that stood up wildly and seemed to be trying to fly from his head. The Japs had given him a rifle and ten pesos and had told him to shoot for the emperor, banzai. He had fired three or four times, but had not hit anything.

His twelve-year-old sister had been watching fearfully. They stood the boy with the back of his head against the tree. Then they knocked in his face with a rifle butt. When Long came up, they were holding a tin cup under his chin to catch the blood. The cup was nearly full.

"What in the name of God is going on here?" cried Long.

"We make her drink it." The man who spoke pointed to the boy's sister who had been forced to stand there.

Long kicked the man in the stomach. "You Jap-brained son of a bitch," he said, "I'll kill you."

There was an angry growl from the crowd. The crowd moved on Long.

"It is an example for the people," they said.

The little girl broke loose and ran. A man ran after her with the cup of blood.

"You stop!" screamed Long. He pointed his gun at the man. "Stop, you bastard, or I'll shoot your guts out."

The man threw the cup at the girl, hitting her and splattering her. She ran on wailing with terror and he turned sullenly to face Long.

"There are going to be court-martials out of this," said Long. "I'll see to that. I'll see that every one of you murderers is tried and convicted after the battle."

"If we live that long."

"You'll live. You bastards will live all right. I don't know why, for God sakes, but bastards like you always live through anything."

Long took the boy to a doctor himself. He wanted to make sure the doctor would treat him, but the boy was already dead. Long listened to his heart himself to make sure.

All the Japs, 110 of them, fell back from the three columns into the town's schoolhouse, which had concrete walls six feet thick to keep the heat out. They took their mortars with them and machine guns and a radio and four prostitutes. They used the radio to ask for reinforcements. Airplanes came and bombed and strafed. Airplanes came every day, but they couldn't do themselves much good. There was too much jungle around there for them.

At two-thirty every morning one of the guerrillas would sneak into the church and set the church bell ringing while everybody else fired one shot. That was to make the Japs think it was a signal for an attack and use up their ammunition shooting all over the place. The Japs bit every time. They shot wildly for hours at every ricochet of one of their own bullets. But they had plenty of ammunition.

On the evening of the second day, the Zapantas wheeled their cannon into place. They spent all night, a whole excited crowd of them with everybody giving advice, aiming the cannon. There were no sights or calibrations on the cannon. They had to aim it by raising the trail with flat rocks. They waited for dawn to make sure everything was just right. Then everybody fell back and Mrs. Zapanta took the lanyard and pulled it. There was the biggest explosion ever heard on earth. The cannon leaped high into the air from the recoil, turned a complete somersault, landed on its barrel, then flipped over and began to bounce. It bounced so far back, Mrs. Zapanta had to run, but the shell had gone right through the six feet of concrete wall, tearing a hole a foot in diameter and banging concrete fragments into the Japs behind it. The Japs could be heard moaning and whimpering all day, but every time anybody showed himself they fired.

The gun was out of commission for two days after that. In the meantime, the guerrillas were busy taking all the supplies they needed in town. The Japs had used many of the houses to billet their men, and there were bodegas scattered everywhere. Major Dongalio made a dash across a cleared space and got into the municipal building. He forced the safe in the treasurer's office and got ninety thousand pesos real money and one hundred thousand Jap pesos. Then he found cases of Jap cigarettes. He threw them out the window across the cleared space to where his men were hiding. But by the time he made the dash back, most of the cigarettes had vanished.

After midnight on the fifth day, Long brought his men up close to the schoolhouse for a dawn assault to be synchronized with the second shell from the cannon. They hoped to get across the cleared space around the schoolhouse under the cover of night, lay low until the shell passed over their heads, then dash into the schoolhouse on top of it. The Japs had turkeys staked out in the clearing to serve as watchdogs. Long's men shot the turkeys the afternoon of the fourth day and early in the evening Long crawled into the clearing and got them. Then they all had turkey dinner together.

At first light, with dawn only minutes away, Long gave the signal and started creeping for the clearing. Looking around, he found only a few men following him. The rest were hanging back. It was very hard to see there. It was still quite dark. Finally Long made out eight men standing in single file behind one palm tree. They were all trying to keep the one tree between them and the Japs.

Long waded into them with his shoes and gun butt, and hammered them out towards the clearing.

Then he ran around looking for more, but before he could find any, wham! the cannon went off and the Japs started firing back. There was only one man in the clearing, a fourteen-year-old boy. The Japs hit him. Long ran out and dragged his dead body to safety. Then the attack was over.

There could not be another. The barrel of the Zapanta cannon had peeled back like a banana. One of the prostitutes in the schoolhouse told the guerrillas later that if they had fired one more shell, the Japs would have surrendered.

The guerrillas now started to burn the town. Japs needed towns to live off. Towns made good collecting points for food, and Jap garrisons were always based in towns. All the people had run away from the fighting and to keep them from returning the guerrillas burned down every building and house in town except the concrete ones. Those they dynamited.

On the seventh day, Jap reinforcements came and the guerrillas withdrew with two motor launches and a whole wagon train of supplies.

The battle taught an important lesson in guerrilla tactics: Never attack a town; firing on troops in entrenched positions wastes too much ammunition.

Long looked very well when I saw him. His face bore no marks from Gidoka, and the scars on his sunburned legs looked hardly more than deeper streaks of sunburn.

"I don't sleep so well when I have nothing to do," he said. "I think too much. When I have something to do, I don't think at all but just do it and then I sleep like a baby."

He told me he had put together the best combat company of guerrillas in the Philippines. "I have weeded out all the slow joes. My boys are as good as the best in the United States Army." They had been working in malaria country and their Atabrine had been short. "I thought of something to save on Atabrine and tried it out on myself," he said. "I dissolved one Atabrine pill in five cc. of water and then put it in me with a needle. It knocked hell out of

154

the fever, the one pill did, and saved me using all that regular dose." He was very proud of that.

Long had come down to the submarine for supplies. His next mission was to hold a river. There were no jungle paths along there, and if he could deprive the Japs of the river they would have to go miles around to keep contact between their garrisons.

The last I saw of Long, he was slouching along with his men, so sunburned and wild-haired that he looked very nearly like one of them.

"So long, kid," I called. He was younger than I.

"Keep punching." He waved back at me with his Garand.

The mission was very dangerous. The only way he had to patrol the river was by baroto. There was place for ambush all up and down the whole length of that damned river, and I never heard of Long again. I don't know whether he's alive or dead. Long Tom Baxter, United States Army Air Force. I sure hope he's alive. He was living on borrowed time the last I saw him, but I sure hope his credit continues good forever. He had a wonderful smile. It was the kind of smile that takes over your heart completely and at once.

23

Well, Parsons had said to me, the navy is jumping up and down for intelligence and they're jumping up and down on me so I'm jumping up and down on you. I told them I had a red-hot young naval officer up here and then you let me down. Well, are you, or what? Are you a red-hot naval officer, or what are you? What MacArthur wants is intelligence. He's red-hot on that. He's got a one-track mind on that. So that's what I want you to get on the ball right away, and get red-hot on right away.

I started for Leyte December 1. Fertig's boys had taken our launch away. Fertig said the subs were going to come in regularly now with supplies and he needed it. He was boss. I had to steal a banca for transportation. I wrote Fertig a luke-cool note explaining I had stolen it and if any banca owner came hollering to him, please to settle with him.

There was equipment to add on to what I already had, giving me three radio sets in all, one master set and two feeders. There were nine of us aboard the banca, five soldiers and Lt. Joe Rifareal, who knew radio, myself and two banca men. We had four carbines, two tommy guns, and five rifles. We tried to keep out of the shipping lanes. We spent a night and most of the next day not going anywhere. Then a wind came up and we went spanking and spatting along. We had to bail the boat every five minutes. I was worried about the radio equipment. I had covered it with raincoats, but the raincoats weren't very good.

We had no sleep the rest of that day and all the next night, just spanking and spatting along, and all hands

156

bailing every five minutes on account of the radio equipment. The wind fell off finally. It fell flat as your hand. There wasn't a breath stirring all day, and we sat motionless in the bay, baking there and hoping a Jap ship would not happen along. We tried to get some sleep. I put a blanket over me, but the sun cooked right through it. You could feel the heat nibbling through your sunburn looking for more skin underneath to burn. Then we'd wake up every few minutes and look for ships. If we had seen one, there wouldn't have been anything for us to do about it, but we looked anyway.

That night about midnight we got about three kilometers from the mainland, but the current was against us. We fought the current a long while. Then, just when it was starting to get light, we made out a big Jap launch. On the tack we were then making, our courses would converge.

I called all hands to general quarters. That meant distributing ourselves over the deck and lying down on it. The bulwark along the side extended about six inches above the deck and we pressed as flat as we could, keeping our rifles by our side. Timonel on the tiller and the two men of the banca crew on the outriggers were then the only ones the Japs could see unless they came very close.

Then I ordered the course changed. I didn't want to converge, but I didn't want to get astern of the Jap launch either. That way, they could have killed all of us with a single burst of their .50 caliber machine guns forward in the pilothouse. What I wanted was to pass broadside to, enabling all our guns to be brought to bear and giving us maximum target angle. I gave the orders lying flat there and speaking into the deck so my voice would not carry over the water.

The launch passed about four hundred yards from us. It was light enough by then to see quite a few Japs aboard. I think that may have been why the launch did not stop to investigate. They were overloaded already. They couldn't handle prisoners if they found them.

There was a funny smell in the air. I didn't know anything for sure, but I didn't like a Jap launch overloaded with troops going out of the regular shipping lanes. It gave a Jap smell to the air. I stopped trying to put the banca against the current without wind onto the mainland and went to Limasawa. I was in a hurry anyway to get to Leyte and send a telegraph message to Heminway to come on the double to Burgos, where we were intending to land the radio equipment.

Rifareal remained in charge of the banca and the radio stuff and I got into a baroto. It took from ten o'clock until three to get to the beach near Burgos. The current was very harmful. I would paddle fifty strokes on the right side, then bail very fast in order not to lose to the current all the ground gained, then paddle fifty strokes on the left side and bail again. Once I was nearly swamped. I could not stop for a minute's rest in the five hours.

I got into Burgos about three-thirty. I still had eighteen kilometers to go to Malitbog. I stopped a civilian on a bicycle.

"Here are two pesos, genuine money," I said.

"Sir, my wife is having a baby, only."

"She can't have it on a bicycle."

"Sir, I will have much to run."

"You will have legs to run." I took my tommy gun off my back with my right hand and held out the two pesos with my left. "You had better take the money."

"Oh, sir. It does not please me, sir."

He took the money. I wasn't fooling. The more I smelled the air, the less I liked it. I don't know what it was, a tension sort of, or something.

I laid the tommy gun across the handlebars and cinched my pack. I made the eighteen kilometers in about an hour. Curly wasn't at the Casa. There wasn't anybody there. It was locked up. I went over to the Villa where Don Augustine—Don Lorenzo's brother—lived. Teting was there.

"The Japs are coming," he said.

"When?" I remember I did not even feel surprised.

"When did they, or when will they?"

"As you want, whatever you want to say. Say it though, fast, fast."

"They came before, and now we think they will come again, to stay."

"Did they take Curly?"

"No, but it is thought that they will when they come again, so she went to attend her cousin's wedding."

"And nobody knows more?"

"Only that they came before and will come again soon to stay."

While I had been at the sub, word had come that the Japs were on a hunt for abacá fiber to make rope. Don Lorenzo had two to three hundred picles of it in his warehouse. A picle is sixty pounds. The guerrillas had taken it out of the warehouse adjoining the Casa and burned it. It was still burning two days later when the Japs arrived.

They came in two small transports. A captain and ten soldiers headed straight for the Casa. Curly met them at the entrance to give Pop Warner and Frank Laird and Mike Americh time to duck out the back and get to the hills.

The captain spoke English well. "Who are you?" he asked.

Curly told him.

"So you are the one who is in love with the Americano, Major Richardson?"

Curly did not answer.

"Are you?" The smirk went off the captain's face. He became stern.

"Is that a subject of official inquiry?" asked Curly.

"You like Americanos?"

Curly did not reply. She stood quietly. She gave the Jap her most imposing manner. It is very imposing.

"You like white faces that look like boiled pork?"

"Is it among the duties of his Emperor's officers to insult women?"

The Jap then began to search the house. He opened the door of each bedroom and stood while his soldiers poked in the drawers and closets and turned the beds, and lifted the rugs. Curly followed. She had mementoes of me in her bedroom, a photograph, a major's oak leaf, and, worst of all, a box full of my notes on the guerrilla movement. I had given them to her for safekeeping when I had gone off to the sub.

Curly's bedroom is the first in the north wing. When the Japs reached the door, Curly said quietly, "That's only my bedroom." She said it as though she expected the captain to respect her privacy, and they passed on.

When they came to the room in which Mike had been sleeping, they found a box of tools and opened it. Lettered on the inside of the lid was "Sgt. Gordon Smith, AUS, La Junta, Colorado."

"Who is this man?" The captain was all bristling again.

"He went to Mindanao to leave on a submarine. He left his address to have the box sent to him after the war."

The Jap was unbristling a little, but the nastiness began to rise in him again.

"You're too good for Filipinos? You must go with Americanos?" he asked and he said, "It is too bad you are rich. If you were not, you would collect the ten thousand pesos reward for Major Richardson.

"Why did you burn the abacá?" he said.

"Would I burn my uncle's abacá? The guerrillas took it from our bodega. They burned it."

When the Japs finally left, Curly went into the kitchen.

"My goodness," she said, "I would like so much a cup of tea."

"My goodness!" was the strongest exclamation she ever used.

24

The next day, December 6, the typhoon came. I was supposed to go to Burgos to meet Heminway and the radio equipment, but it was too dangerous to move. Coconuts and whole trees were whirling through the air like armor-piercing shells. This was the typhoon through which the Japs moved to wipe out Miranda, at "Camp Heaven."

When the typhoon subsided, Major Francesco, who was to take my place as chief of staff of the guerrilla army when I concentrated on the radio network, started to drive me to Burgos. But there were too many trees down and a bridge had been washed out. I continued on bicycle.

Our radio equipment was safe. Rifareal had made the beach with it five minutes before the typhoon broke and had got the stuff into a building where the winds and rain had not harmed it. Heminway was there while we looked the stuff over, hopping from one foot to the other. One set was missing.

"Oh sir, yes sir. We forgot to tell you, sir. They came in a launch and took it."

"Who took it? What launch?"

"The Americanos, sir, before we left."

Then I found out that, of all the Goddam luck in the world, they had failed to put in the engine and generator for the biggest set, the master set.

"What the hell are you hopping around like that for?" I asked Heminway.

"Well," he said, "for the last three nights—"

"Is this a long story?"

"It's kind of not very long."

"Is it funny? By this time I need a funny story."

"No sir, it's not very funny."

161

He and St. John had been sitting around with Kitty waiting for the baby. Kitty had been complaining of pains for three days. They had a nurse up from Maasin. The nurse would bellyache about being there for nothing, but every time she got ready to go the pains would start up in Kitty again.

"I've been walking the floor three nights," said Heminway. "I'm a nervous wreck."

"How about Kitty?"

"Oh, she's fine. She's a healthy kid. Women can take those things better than men, anyway."

"That's pretty thoughtful of the Lord," I said, "since they're the ones who generally have to take it."

"Yes, that's so, but gee, I'm a nervous wreck. Then this morning Kitty kept walking around and around and I kept walking around and around with her. St. John sat over in a corner drinking tuba. Then the baby came. I was so surprised. It just came.

" 'Johnny,' I said, 'hey, Johnny, come over and take a look.'

" 'Not me,' Johnny said. 'No sir, this beats the hell out of me.'

"But it just came, and that's all there was to it."

"Okay, now let's get the stuff set up."

"But I have to get home and get my clothes and stuff and gee, I've got a kid. He was just born."

It ended up that I put up the radio station with Joe Rifareal. It was the first and only time that any guerrilla enterprise that I had anything to do with worked right off the bat. We put the radio set in a house by the side of the road. We cut the antenna according to the formula for our frequency, stretched it between two coconut trees, put in the lead-in and the ground, hooked up the batteries, and we were on the air. But the message I sent went snafu anyway. Fertig didn't get it for two days. Something was wrong at the other end. They had their own troubles down there.

When I woke up the next morning the guard told me a launch had passed by about four o'clock. "Godspeed the bastards," I said. Then Heminway arrived about seven-thirty in the morning. He was panting a little bit.

"We had the christening this morning," he said. He always started a story 'way in back of the day before yesterday and I listened patiently. "St. John and Kitty and myself, we took the baby to the church about six o'clock. I carried the baby."

"Who carried Kitty?"

"Oh, she walked. She's fine. She says she could have a baby every day if it weren't for the other things taking so long. Then, while the priest was talking, right in the most important part, holy cats! I held out my hand and looked at it. I couldn't help it. The baby had christened me. The priest looked at me like a teacher, just like when you do something wrong in school, but it wasn't me, it was the baby. The baby had christened me.

"After that happened, the priest made everything extra slow and solemn to restore the dignity sort of. Then somebody busted in. There was a Jap launch pulling in to the dock a couple hundred yards from the church."

I turned and began to walk fast towards the house where we had our radio. I knew if the Japs had come there, they would come everywhere.

"Hey, don't you want to hear the rest of it?" Heminway came running after me. " 'Prrrrp, prrrrp, prrrp, finished!' said the priest, running all the Latin together. He knew St. John and I had to hurry. I gave him a dollar and gave the baby to Kitty, and St. John and I went tearing out of there. He's a nice baby. He didn't cry a bit."

The Japs landed all over everywhere that day. They took every one of our towns—Inopacan, Hilongos, Bato, Maasin, Macrahon, Malitbog, Sogod, Cabalian, Anahawan, Hinundayan, Hinunangan—all on Leyte—and Liloan and Pintuyan on Panoan Island across the bay.

The southern Leyte guerrillas had begun to itch the hide of them. They reached out fingers to squash us. When Heminway went across the bay to Panoan Island, there were Jap launches all over. He had a platform in his banca twelve inches high to keep cargo out of the water that collected on deck. The platform saved Heminway's life. He squeezed himself under it and lay in the bilge water.

Once the Japs came alongside and inspected the banca, but the Filipino crew looked ordinary and Heminway lay without sound or motion even when the stinking bilge water covered over his face.

25

The Japs landing in southern Leyte found no army to oppose them. They came charging up the beach, threw their machine guns down, threw themselves down. The people stared at them curiously.

Where are the guerrillas?

No understand.

You understand. Where are the guerrillas?

They are gone.

Where have they gone?

Back there, sir.

Well, we have come to rescue you from them.

Oh, thank you, sir.

We have come to liberate you from the bandits.

Oh, sir, you flatter us, you despise us, you are too good to us only, sir.

It is our pleasure to welcome good neighbors into the Greater East Asia Co-Prosperity Sphere.

Viva Hapons! Banzai!

Now, where are the guerrillas?

They are gone, sir.

Where have they gone?

Oh, sir, back there only.

Will you help us to find them and thus aid your own liberation from the bandits?

Oh, sir, who can find the guerrillas? They are gone only. There is no finding them.

The Japs fanned out into the hills. We watched their columns walking along staring curiously at our pop bottle telegraph system. Their columns converged on nothing. Their pincers clutched empty air. Not a shot was fired at them. They found nothing to shoot at. A fifth columnist would tell where a headquarters house was. T

would surround it stealthily at night. They would rush it at
night. They would find a sleepy man and his sleepy wife
and sleepy children.

Where are the guerrillas?

Oh, sir, they are gone.

Where have they gone?

Back there only.

You must not hide the guerrillas. It is death for you
and your children to hide them.

Oh, sir, we do not hide them. They come with guns.
We have no guns. They stay with guns. We have no guns
to make them leave. Then you come with guns and they
leave.

Where did they go?

Oh sir, who knows where a guerrilla goes?

And when necessary, a guerrilla could go into the
earth. He would put his gun under leaves, take up a tool,
and be a farmer.

Oh, yes sir, I live here, sir.

Oh, yes sir, he is my cousin only, sir. He works for
me, sir, very good.

The Japs developed a saying every time they saw a
husky young farmer: farm boy by day, guerrilla by night.

Oh, no sir, you do not understand, sir. I wish peace
only, sir.

Kangleon without any guns to repel strong forces,
without ammunition enough to fight pitched battles, was
waging a canny war. It was a war that did not exist for a
long time. He had seven hundred men in this sector, about
half of them with rifles. The Japs hunted them with more
than five thousand heavily armed troops, a completely
equipped task force. We had lost all our transportation in
the landings, all our installations, our fuel distillery, our
telegraph communications, our ordnance plant, our government, but we had not lost a single man or a single
bullet. Kangleon knew eventually the Japs would tire of
sending their columns on long forced marches through
thin air. The force would be too expensive to maintain
doing nothing with guerrilla armies active on other islands.
The Japs would start to withdraw it. Kangleon could not
wait until they withdrew altogether. For political reasons,

there must be a fight. The people had supported a guerrilla army. It must fight for them. Else, how would hope of liberation be kept alive until MacArthur arrived? If hope of liberation died altogether, what would MacArthur do for intelligence? What force would there be to aid him when he landed? No, there must be a fight. But not where it would be suicide. Not when the Japs were at their strongest. Nor when they were at their weakest either, when they had withdrawn into the towns and too much ammunition would be required to get at them. The guerrillas must strike at a time in between, when the Japs were not so weak that they were no longer sending out patrols but not so strong that their patrols were columns.

So the Jap columns marched up and down and we watched them, sullenly or fearfully according to our temperament, but whatever our temperament we watched silently. The only action was when the Japs started to use our pop bottle telegraph. We cut the line. They repaired it. We chopped down the trees. They strung the line from other trees. We took down ten kilometers of wire in a single night. They gave up telegraphing.

The Japs marched sternly into the Casa and began questioning Don Lorenzo, the head of the family and of the numerous Escano enterprises. Don Lorenzo is a gray-haired, well-built, faultlessly tailored man in his middle fifties. He was one of sixteen children. All his brothers and sisters had numerous offspring. Curly's mother, who was Don Lorenzo's sister, had herself had sixteen children. The family was closely knit like a corporate enterprise with branches. Don Lorenzo was a descendant of Castilian Jews. His home had fine silverware and expensive china enough to serve dinner for one hundred and twenty-five people at once. It was equipped with Electrolux iceboxes and a Scott radio that cost six thousand pesos.

You were friendly with Americans, the Japs said, you opened your house to them.

They walked in armed.

You opened your house to the guerrillas.

They were armed. The door of my house was opened to you, too. You are armed.

Joe and Teting Escano are guerrillas.

The young are inflamed by the times. I am neutral. I am a businessman. The world for me is made up of customers whom I seek to serve so that they may serve me.

You gave the guerrillas three hundred sacks of rice and twenty sacks of dried fish.

They were armed.

We are armed, too.

I have no more rice and I have no more fish. You came with your arms too late.

But you have cash.

I have cash and you are armed.

We will take the rice and fish in cash.

Don Lorenzo gave them four thousand pesos.

While their columns still hunted the hills, the Japs were like this to all the people in the towns, firm but cautious and reasonable robbers. Then they descended on Union and summoned all the people of the town to a meeting. The mayor was made responsible for all the people being there. The Kempetai—a kind of Japanese Gestapo—searched the houses to make sure none had refrained from attending.

A speech was made, a good neighbor speech and a Greater East Asia Co-Prosperity speech. Then the women and children were sent home, and all the males—about two hundred of them—were marched into a little one-room schoolhouse. The Jap soldiers marched in, the Kempetai and the town's fifth columnists. Among the men in that room were two guerrilla officers and five guerrilla soldiers. They had wandered into town curious to see what the meeting would be like. Everybody knew their identity except the Japs, the Kempetai, and the fifth columnists.

The men were kept in the room for two days and nights. The air became very foul. Some of the older ones and those with malaria fainted. There was no room to lie down. There was hardly room to stand. A man who sat down would have to sit with his legs under him. If he spread out his legs, he would have a fight with his neighbor. That was one of the torments of the confinement, how tempers frayed and spirits broke down. At first the prisoners sang. They thought they were going to be killed and they sang together. But as the body wore down, the mind wore down, too. There was no food, no water, no air, no sanitation facilities, no sleep. The poisons of fatigue nagged at the mind and nibbled and frayed and broke it. The singing stopped. Quarreling began. When, the second day, the Japs thrust in a small pail of water, only the men around the door got any of it.

On the third day the Kempetai and the Jap soldiers returned. Instantly spirit came back into the prisoners. They were solid again against the Japs. Those who were not inclined that way by courage knew that one day the Japs would leave and then the guerrillas would return and kill them if they had talked.

The Japs tried the salt-water treatment. They tied a man's hands and feet and ran the cord around his neck so that if he struggled he would strangle himself. Then they forced a wedge into his mouth to hold it open, held his nose, and poured sea water into his mouth. He had to swallow to breathe. If he did not swallow, he would suffocate. He had all the sensations of drowning. And if he swallowed the sea water, his abdomen would distend painfully and would distend more and more as the water continued endlessly coming.

The Japs learned the identity of the soldiers they had captured. They took them to Malitbog to submit them to further treatment to get more information. A man led the Japs to Major Francesco's headquarters—a house in the hills. He led them along a path where he knew an outpost had been stationed. The outpost blew his bojong, and the Japs surrounded and stormed into an empty house.

Then the Japs shot and killed anybody they found with a bojong. The volunteer guards took to sending signals with smudge fires. The Japs shot and killed anybody they found building a smudge fire. Finally they shot and killed anybody they found near a smudge fire.

The volunteer guards stopped building smudge fires. They learned to hoot with their mouths like owls. The Japs could not shoot and kill anybody they found with a mouth. Not then, anyway. Not yet awhile.

26

Fertig had promised Kangleon a radio set, and I delivered it to him and set it up for him. I told him my mission was now intelligence. I had a network to put in and operate. We were to be in touch with each other. He would feed his intelligence to Souwespac through me. He would provide me with soldiers to defend my stations.

About the soldiers, they seldom materialized. Sometimes Kangleon said he could not spare them. Every rifle was needed to kill Japs. MacArthur did not care if I killed one or a thousand Japs, what he wanted out of me was intelligence. But Kangleon cared if he killed Japs. He had his own problems. MacArthur's requests were only one of them. If Kangleon did not kill Japs, he was lost. Radio stations were likely to be too costly to him in rifles, ammunition, and men. They were too easily located with direction finders. Besides, Kangleon never really set too high a value on the kind of intelligence Souwespac wanted—ship movements, airplane movements, disposition of Jap forces, changes in same. When an enemy's bayonet is at your heart, you do not give as high a priority to a description of him that would help apprehend him later as to killing him at once. So, for the most part, I had to do without rifles and soldiers.

Curly was all right. She was headed off from returning to Malitbog and instead stayed hidden at the home of a cousin.

I gave Heminway two thousand pesos to run his radio station. I set St. John up with two thousand pesos, too. Fertig had given me plenty of money. Rifareal, Sergeant Pedro Paturan, and myself went off to set up the master set.

There was a very steep slope down to the beach. We

went down it at night. There were some Japs sitting out on the beach enjoying themselves. We lay low waiting for them to go away. They had whores with them. We spent a long time discussing how to kill them, but there was no way to retreat running with the radio equipment we had. We knew it would take four hours to paddle across the bay. We needed night. The day would be too dangerous. Finally we agreed the Japs had used too much of the night and we would have to postpone our trip to the next night. We decided to kill the Japs. We lugged the radio stuff back up the hill and then came down the hill to the beach. But the Japs and their whores had gone. So we returned for the equipment, loaded it into a baroto, and paddled. The last hour's paddling was in daylight. We just sweated it out. We hit the beach running, got into the jungle, and lay there all day. Most of the time we slept.

That evening we started into the hills. We had a contact there, and he led us four kilometers up a river and to a ramshackle hill hut. Period. Now all I needed was an engine, a generator, fuel, gasoline, lubricating oil, telephone wire for my lead-in from the engine to the set. I dragooned a guerrilla, a fine boy, Lt. Juanito Baybay, to scrounge up stuff for me. I remembered an engine and generator unit in Sogod, a Fairbanks-Morse that had provided power for a hair-curling machine. A fifth columnist had taken it from the beauty parlor owner who was loyal and had buqweed when the Japs came in. Juanito came in at night and took it from him.

"Later we come back and take your life," he told the fifth columnist.

It required three days to make the round trip. In that time, we went among the civilians there and set up a volunteer guard system and hired helpers, and then camouflaged the trail to our hut, littering the entrance with stones and scattering underbrush over the ruts and footworn parts. The camouflage was a work of art. The Filipinos are very good at it.

The engine turned out to be 110 volts, alternating current. The set needed 220 volts. We worked for five days winding and unwinding trying to step up the voltage. Nothing we did had any luck. The volunteer guards were green then and very nervous.

"I think I see Japs coming." That would be a report.

"What makes you think so?"

"I don't know, sir. I have a feeling. It feels to me they are coming, sir."

"Do not feel. Do not think. Only see. Do not report unless you see."

Then one night: "I think I see Japs coming."

"What makes you think so?"

"Oh, sir, because I see them only, sir."

We moved out. It took twelve men to carry the engine on poles. It took fifteen men to carry a barrel of lubricating oil. There were fifty carriers altogether. We stuck to the jungle, wading down a rocky river. A man would fall and there would be a great straining. A pole would break and there would be more straining. But nobody shouted or even talked loud. We moved as silently as we could, and all that marked our passing was the cockatoos shrieking at us.

It turned out to be a false alarm. I called all the civilian guards together and spoke to them earnestly. "We have lost valuable time," I said. "It is necessary to be brave and be men and not be women seeing a Jap hiding behind every Kalow bird."

They agreed. They would not report the shadows of Japs, only Japs.

Then we had a beautiful stroke of luck. We found a stepped-down transformer which would convert 110 volts into 220. It had been used for the only motion-picture projector in southern Leyte. Rifareal remembered the projector, and suddenly it occurred to him it might have a transformer. Sure enough, it did have and we got it. But then the engine and generator wouldn't work. The magneto had gone out and wouldn't give a spark. We would heat the manifold and heat the carburetor and heat the engine. We'd get everything red-hot. The engine would start to sputter and then die. We'd start over again and it would sputter again and die. It just kept leading us on.

Finally we said the hell with it and all went out among the Japs to look for another engine. We got an International, a one-cylinder horizontal one-half- to two-and-one-half-horsepower engine with two flywheels. It took us two days to mount the engine on hewn logs. We didn't have a brace and bit. To bore holes, we had to heat up a bolt and hammer it through. If you hammered too hard, the bolt bent.

Kangleon had sent a message by runner telling me not to put up the master set. It was too powerful, 100 watts. The Japs would locate it too easily with their direction finders and it was too bulky for me to run away with fast. But I thought, the hell with that. I was too wrapped up in it now to stop.

The engine and generator worked fine. We had two light bulbs in the house. They both went on and we cheered like for a parade. Gee, that was a happy minute. But smoke started to come out of the transmitter, a little at first, but before we could run the short space to it, the smoke was just streaming out. We pulled out the plug and took out the transformer. It had burned out.

It took until the next day to get the transformer back into shape. Fortunately as hell, the trouble was just in the outer layer. A wire had fused there. We unwound it and Rifareal did some hocus-pocus with a piece of paper and there we were, back where we had started from the day before. Our radio operator was Jorge Capillas, a first lieutenant. He made a contact with the press key and we listened to the receiver and heard ourself. Then he adjusted it to exactly our frequency by listening to our receiver and watching the calibration. We listened to Mindanao tensely until they weren't busy. Then we broke in on them. They answered immediately.

This knocked me off my feet. I didn't have a message prepared. I asked how they were receiving us.

"QRK5—QRK5." This is radio ham talk for a powerful, clear signal. We jumped up and down. We ran around hitting each other on the back.

They told us they would start taking our messages at four o'clock. It was about one o'clock then. Our engine started on gasoline. Once it got going we could switch to crude oil for fuel, but it wouldn't start on crude oil. We had used the last of the gasoline starting the engine. I sent runners out to buy more and told Paturan, the engineer, to keep the engine going at all costs. We began sweating out the watch. Since the radio was going anyway, we listened to the news from Radio Chungking. America announced a new propellerless plane that could do seven hundred miles an hour and would be useful in commercial aviation after the war. Madang in New Guinea had been bombed. At three o'clock, the engine stopped. We were out of fuel.

The runners didn't come back until the next day. In the meantime, eleven o'clock that night in the rain a volunteer guard arrived panting to say the Japs were on their way.

"You saw them?"

"I saw them."

"You did not think you saw them, but you saw them with your eyes?"

"Oh, sir, I saw them with my eyes only, sir."

We started disconnecting the wires and boxing up the equipment. We worked all in a tumble. We moved the stuff out about fifty yards into the jungle and covered it with palm leaves. We were still covering it when the Japs arrived, but we didn't lose anything. We had moved everything before starting to cover anything. We finished covering the stuff while the Japs were still there. We could hear them questioning the owner of the house, Vidal.

"You are a friend of the Americano? You help him?"

"He came with guns."

"Where is he?"

"Oh, sir, he is gone only."

"Where did he go?"

"Back in the hills."

"You help us find him?"

"Oh, sir, who can find him? He go into the air."

We had another house prepared for us about a kilometer and a half away. But I decided we'd do the thing right this time, we'd build our own place in the jungle and stay off the air until we got it set. We found a semi-clearing and planted bamboo poles, one for each corner and two in the center. We used palm leaves for the roof and walls and rattan vines to secure them. The floor was bamboo, fresh, green, brand-new bamboo.

We set the radio up when the house had only a wall and a half completed. I was too impatient to wait any longer. Our antenna was about eighty feet up in the trees. One of our boys was an expert tree climber. He could go clear to the top of a tree with nothing to hold on to. He just seemed to walk up with his hands and feet. But when he walked up one where tree ants had made their home, the tree ants beat him off. They are very large. Their teeth bite deep. He couldn't let his hands free to fight them. He had to retreat.

"The Goddamn guerrilla ants," he said.

Then we were set to go. But Mindanao was too busy. We called all day and they wouldn't answer. They answered the next day.

I told them power and fuel troubles had delayed sending. I wouldn't put in about the Japs. I wouldn't put in they had delayed us, too.

They sent us a well done, but that was premature. They should have said BU for balls-up because, Goddammit, there I was with a master set and my receiver was too weak to receive the little old bitty sets St. John and Heminway had! All I could do was transmit the messages I originated.

However, I felt like Christmas anyway. I told Rifareal to go home and see his wife for Christmas, he hadn't seen her for three months. Then I went calling on Curly. I traveled at night. I carried my tommy gun for myself and a bottle of San Miguel, made-in-Manila beer and cigarettes for Curly.

I arrived where she was staying about midnight. I yelled up at the house. Her cousin's wife opened the window.

"Sshhh," she said.

The Kempetai had been bothering them. They had been keeping a watch. I went softly into the house. Curly flew to me.

"What happened?" she cried.

"It's Christmas."

"Is that all that happened?"

"For a good Catholic, that's a hell of a way to talk. What more can happen than Christmas?"

"But it is so dangerous nowadays. There is so much death. There is death for everyone everywhere."

"For me," I said, "there is Christmas," and kissed her.

"Oh, my goodness," she said, and then she said, "for me, too."

Curly put on her best dress. It was a sort of orange red with a lot of white in it. I remember it had little bits of sort of paste puff sleeves and she wore crepe-soled shoes, low-heeled, with canvas tops. She looked so beautiful in the lamplight, she was like the thought of Christmas come to life. Then we walked out into the jungle to find Teting and Major Francesco and the guerrillas and have Christmas with them.

It's hard to tell about that Christmas, the Christmas of 1943, because nothing happened and yet I had such a good time. I don't think I've ever had such a good time. There were fighting cocks all over the headquarters. We arrived about three o'clock in the morning. A cockfight was going on. We breakfasted on the losers. Then we all slept on the floor together. Late in the day Curly and I walked alone. There wasn't much jungle there. It was just sort of cleared land with some trees and little rushing brooks and big hills, all purpled over by the air there in the evening.

Christmas night, Curly said Christmas was over and now it's New Year's Eve. She produced from her pack a bottle of Sailor Boy whisky and a bottle of Old Squire gin, both made in Manila. Curly was always like that. Whatever the circumstances, she was the perfect hostess. We put eggs into the whisky and produced something faintly like a Tom and Jerry. Then she gave me a clever little poem she had painted on abacá cloth with a palm tree on one side of the poem and a beach for the poem to sit on and a little blue ocean for the beach to bathe in. The poem was something about her love, how even if I had not come seeking it, she would have given it to me, and how once given it I must keep it forever, I could not give it away or throw it away.

In the end, Curly stood up with glass in hand. "Welcome, 1944," she cried. "Oh, 1944, please be beautiful to us."

Her face looked so poignant when she said it. The

guerrillas stirred. I remember that. I remember the swarthy, powerful men stirring as if a wind had moved among them, and I remember how beautiful and poignant Curly looked.

81mm Mortar

27

By the end of January, Kangleon deemed the time ripe for the guerrillas to strike. He ordered his men to go over to the offensive at 0000 hours, midnight February 1, 1944, and all through the last night of January regiments and units came slouching down from the hills to take up previously scouted positions outside the towns. There have been armies like that before—George Washington's must have been a good deal like that with soldiers going off to help the wife have a baby or help plant or take in the crop and soldiers running away when the curve pitching started and coming back when hungry, the chow soldiers. We called them "chow soldiers," and whatever George Washington called them it must have meant the same thing, that they were chow soldiers. No, such an army as Kangleon sent down that night to the drowsy, thatched-up and tinned-over, dusty, fusty, salt-smelling, rusty little old coastal barrios and towns they have in southern Leyte has its precedents and has plenty of brothers all over the world these days—China, Russia, Tito's boys, the forest lands of Poland, Greece, the FFI in France, the FI in Belgium. Wherever a fascist conqueror has tried to stand, the people have risen under his feet as guerrillas. That's the human race for you, and the Filipino people take their place big in it, just as big as the biggest.

The offensive was a guerrilla offensive. It didn't consist of fellows going over the top after an artillery barrage. Joe Nazareno had artillery, one 81mm. mortar with five shells and one bazooka gun. He and his fellows went over the top, but the rest didn't even have a machine gun (except later when a Jap plane crashed and I got two guns off it in pretty good shape but no bullets; the bullets had all burned up) and so they just hung near the towns waiting for the Jap patrols to come out. Except at Anahawan. There was a garrison of twelve Japs there. They never went out on patrol, just stayed in town, so the boys went in after them, first cooking up a plan with the mayor. They had found one unexploded hand grenade. That was the basis of the plan.

The mayor invited the garrison to breakfast with him the morning of February 1. All came except one. They left him outside as guard. Then the mayor told the Japs he had something special for them in the yard outside, and would go out to get it.

When he came out, that was the signal for the guerrillas to begin. Some had already crawled in close to the house with the hand grenade. One wandered over to the guard. The guerrilla was wearing a play shirt, the tail of it hanging down over his trousers. Under the shirt, stuck in his belt, he had a revolver, all loaded and cocked. He carried in his two hands a live chicken with a string around its leg, a peg at the end of the string. He held the chicken out dumbly to the guard. The Jap motioned to him to take the chicken to the feast inside. The kid acted as if he didn't understand. The Jap made gestures and tried all the sign language and pidgin English he knew. The kid dropped the chicken and the Jap clucked his tongue vexedly and stooped over to grab the peg and stick it in the ground. He didn't like to see the chicken go to waste.

When the kid dropped the chicken, the other guerrillas pulled the pin on the grenade and held it, counting. When the Jap stooped over for the chicken, the kid pulled out his revolver and shot the Jap in the back of the neck, and the others tossed the grenade into the open window of the house and rushed into the house with their rifles on top of the explosion. The bullet was a .45. The bullet penetrated the base of the cranium, glanced off the backbone, and came out through the Jap's belly. Three of the Japs had been out back in the lean-to kitchen, fooling around there. They got away, running, but the rest didn't and our boys got gas masks and some clothes in pretty good shape after washing and sewing, a couple of wristwatches, fine shoes, rifles with quite a bit of ammunition, a Knee mortar with a case of grenades, and three hand grenades.

Joe Nazareno, all flushed up over having the 81mm. mortar and the five shells for it, tried to take his boys into the town of Liloan. He had a combat company with sixty automatic rifles. Kangleon had given him almost every automatic rifle in the army. They came in on two sides.

Doc Parado led one small, diversionary column through the coconut trees. Doc was carrying with him the last rubber glove in southern Leyte. He had been saving it

"Knee Mortar"

for more than eight months to deliver his wife's first baby. He carried it with him in the attack for luck. It will deliver all the Parados safely, he felt. Joe Nazareno led the main force up the beach.

The battle started with a mortar shell that landed just outside the Liloan school building where the Jap garrison was staying. The Japs came piling out into foxholes. They had barbed-wire entanglements, too. It was just too much for Joe's boys. They fought all day. The Japs tried counter-attacks and encircling movements through the coconut trees, but they were held in and chewed up. Our side had two dead and three wounded by the time twilight came. They hadn't been able to use the mortar again. When you have only four shells left, you don't waste them. You wait until the Japs bunch up. But the Japs didn't bunch up.

The Japs had fired star shells, and Joe reasoned that meant a plea for reinforcements from Cabalian, across the Liloan Straits. He held the beach. He fought to hold it and he held it. A banca full of Japs came sneaking over the water at night. Joe and his boys were waiting for them. They waited until the banca grounded on the beach. Then they opened up with everything they had. They had counted about eighty Japs in the banca, all flocked together when the guerrillas opened fire. But Joe's boys dove all night for bodies and rifles and supplies, and when morning came they had found only twenty-five bodies. They were anxious to recover the dead to get the clothes off them, particularly the shoes, and also the cartridge belts. Some of the bodies may have been weighted and carried out to sea by the tide. I don't see how any—or anyway, many—could have got away.

Joe fought a naval battle, too. Reinforcements came that day and drove him off the beach. But Joe sneaked in the next morning and dove for what might have been left around the banca. They found more rifles and a nice little battery radio which was no good any more, but had good spare parts for me. Then the Japs sent a patrol out in a banca. They worked along close to shore, and Joe opened up on them with an unnerving fire. They turned and tried to run. Joe and a crowd of the boys chased after them in a banca of their own. The Japs panicked altogether. There was some maneuvering, but the Japs maneuvered just like chickens with their heads off and gave Joe a line-astern shot and he just mowed them down. Some of them started jumping wildly over the side and some of them started throwing their equipment overboard. The guerrillas took every one of them out of the water to get their shoes.

The bazooka had been set up to command Liloan Straits, connecting Cabalian Bay and Sogod Bay. It had to wait until February 10 to get a shot in. There were no targets. The Japs were too busy fighting off attacks to move around. Then a launch came along, making about eight knots with a five-knot current to step its speed up. It was somewhere about fifty or seventy-five yards offshore. The boys led the target as if firing with a rifle. They had never fired a bazooka before. There were not enough shells to waste on target practice. They aimed for the engine, leading it a little bit and then pressed the trigger and then there was this startling and, to them, unexpected whoooosh.

"It didn't work," said the one who pressed the trigger.

"It fired. It worked," cried the other. "It worked good."

"No, it didn't. I didn't hear it. It's still in there, stuck in the barrel." He pressed the trigger again and again. Nothing, naturally, happened. "It's broken," he shouted and kept pressing the trigger frantically.

Then there was an explosion in the water fifty yards the other side of the Jap launch. The Japs all ran to the far side and looked astonished at the cascade of water. It had been a delayed-action shell for use against tanks. Because they had led the target, not having experience with high-velocity shells, only with rifles, the missile had hit forward of the engine, had gone through one side of the launch just above the water line, plowed through some sacks of rice, passed through the other side, and exploded harmlessly out in the sea. When last seen, the launch was still proceeding with the current at better than eight knots and the Japs were desperately stuffing bags and clothing into the holes in the sides.

There was a long post-mortem on the shot. They wanted to get it right the next time. But there was no next time. The Japs never put a launch through Liloan Straits again. They preferred to go more than sixty miles out of their way rather than risk it.

Then the planes came, bombing and strafing. They plowed up the jungles good. One of them, a two-engined bomber, zigged instead of zagged and ran head-on into a hill. That was the one I got the two machine guns out of, but no bullets. They bombed flat four houses that I had been in with my radio station, but they didn't come near my new setup in the jungle. They hadn't been able to find out about it. The only result of the bombing was that I lost all my civilian workers for about a week. Their wives came and dragged them off to build foxholes for them and the children.

The Japs sent heavy-weapons squads out with their patrols. The guerrillas let them go by. Then, in the evening when the Japs came dragging back all loose and tired from maybe a fifteen-mile march on which they had found nothing, the guerrillas hit them. The country around the towns was not ideal for ambushes. For the ideal ambush, you need a long, deep ravine on the tops of which your troops can stand and fire down from both sides. That's heaven. That's the dream. You need it long so that you can let the whole Jap column get into it before firing. That prevents them from deploying and coming in on one section of your split-up forces. You need it deep so that your own people won't hit into each other when they fire. In the flat country around the towns, the best plan was to form a rough semicircle around the head of the Jap column, the ends of the semicircle running down the sides of the column. In that way the guerrilla commander could keep contact with his troops and they wouldn't fire into each other. The troops retreated individually as they ran short on ammunition, and there was always a rendezvous point selected in advance, at which the troops would collect and make off in a body.

There is no accurate figure on Jap losses. Certainly they ran into the hundreds and perhaps eventually into the thousands. Major Francesco had a blackboard in his headquarters as a morale builder on which he chalked up the totals for the day, week, month, and whole campaign. But guerrillas seldom win and take over battlefields. They shoot until out of ammunition or until the enemy is successfully deployed. Then they retreat. If you don't take battlefields, you can't get an accurate count on dead. Soldiers who see the enemy drop when they fire with a bead on him never consider they missed, and the man might only be ducking. They count him hit. Soldiers who hit a man count him dead. And soldier tales grow, particularly when girls are listening.

Whatever the Jap losses were, it was enough to make them react with brute ferocity. The people of the towns ran frightened into the hills. That made the Jap food position in the towns serious. Their garrisons were living off the townspeople. They were forcing them to work. The Japs could not exist in deserted barrios. They went into the hills with fifth columnists, hunting the evacuees, those who had buqweed. When the fifth columnist identified a buqwee family as townsfolk, it was compelled to return home. The hill families were killed to keep them from aiding guerrillas. The hill barrios were burned to keep guerrillas from living off them. There was no exception to this. Every hill family found was wiped out, not shot because the Japs had an ammunition supply problem, too, but bayoneted or, when there were large numbers and there was not time, cremated in their own burning homes.

I myself watched helpless while the Japs in force burned four barrios. That was why we fought close to the coastal towns rather than pick the more advantageous ambush spots in the hills for our battlefields. We wanted to fight the Japs back out of the hills to save the barrios and save the people there and keep the Japs bottled up in the towns. We knew they wouldn't kill the people they were living off.

The people reacted magnificently. Buqweeing out of the towns was a big help to us. It was the same kind of business that licked Napoleon in Russia. Like the Russians of 1812 Moscow, the Filipino townspeople did it because they were afraid. They were afraid mostly because they just didn't like Japs. But when they buqweed, they forced the Jap's hand and made him send out searching parties which we could hit. There were hundreds of heroes among them. Oh, that story will never be told the way it should be. It is so long. Its chapters are so numerous and so many of them happened in such lonely places where the only witnesses were those who were soon to be dead and their Jap murderers. The hill barrio men took to carrying two bolos. An ordinary bolo has a blade about twelve inches long and is carried on a strap over the shoulder. They carried this and then they carried a small bolo under their shirts. When they were caught and couldn't run—the Japs were willing to spend a bullet on a running man—they'd drop their big bolos as ordered and wait until the Japs came close to tie them up. Then they'd snatch the small bolo out from under their shirts and work with it until killed. It finally got so the Japs wouldn't go near a prisoner until he had first taken off his shirt. Then the Filipinos took to carrying shards of glass in their mouths, razor blades if they could find them and sharpened nails to strike enemy eyes—anything that would do damage and keep a man from feeling he was a dumb beast standing mutely waiting to be killed.

And the civilians planted mine fields against the Japs, their kind, the best kind they could get. They took a type of bamboo called bagakay, long, slender, wet, and poisonous, and made it into suak, which are double-edged barbs. They say it's poisonous. Anyway, if you cut your hand on it, the cut festers. The natives hate to work with it, but they made thousands of barbs and planted them along the trails Jap patrols took, concealing them very artfully in the grass. Then, when a patrol came along, they'd fire a shot or, if they had no guns, just shout and the Japs would drop flat against the suak. When the Japs knew where the suak was, the natives would transplant it. It worked. I saw hundreds of suak barbs with Jap blood on them.

Very slowly and desperately and bloodily, Kangleon's army fought the Japs back into the coastal towns. The Japs couldn't send for reinforcements. When reinforcements came, they had no fighting to do. The guerrillas would lay low. They'd just hit when the patrols were weak, and finally there were no more patrols. The Japs didn't dare leave the coast. They yielded the hills to us. But that was a long time happening. It had to wait until an American submarine came in with help for us.

28

Jap headquarters for southern Leyte were at the Casa in Malitbog. Joe and Teting Escano led the fight there. That was their home. Their hearts were in it. Joe sat guarding the southern approaches to the town. Teting held the north. He disposed his forces just north of a bridge over a stream that cut the main provincial highway to the town of Sogod. A Jap patrol of about thirty came out. Teting waited until they were on the bridge. Then he let them have it, and killed eight.

The Japs deployed along the southern bank of the river. They tried to wade across. That cost them some more lives—how many is not certain. When you fire at a wading man, he goes under the water whether you hit him or not.

Then the Japs tried to bust across the bridge in a truck. They had one truck with armor plate to protect the engine and sandbags to protect the men in the truck. Teting was ready for that. He had high-velocity "Double O" buckshot fired down from on high. It burst among the Japs like shrapnel.

After that the Japs brought up mortars. They worked over both Joe and Teting with mortars. But both boys had foxholes ready. They had a first line of foxholes and a second line. They dropped back or came forward from line to line depending on what the Japs were ranging on. Those were good commanders. Yes, they were both very good commanders and they had it so that, finally, the Japs never dared leave Malitbog except by launch.

The Japs held a meeting for the population of Malitbog like the one they had held in Union. They kept all the males in the church for three days. Then they walked them out into the courtyard. A convent overlooked the courtyard. A woman sat in a window there behind some mosquito netting. All the males were walked past her singly. They couldn't make out who she was, only that she was a woman. She identified for the Japs who among the civilians had helped the guerrillas and who hadn't. She just held one hand up. When a guerrilla sympathizer walked by, she lowered her hand silently and the man was taken out of line for the sea water treatment. She identified Manuelito Escano, Curly's brother, as Captain Campos, a guerrilla leader. He does look something like Campos. She identified Ed Escano, another of Curly's brothers, as one who had aided the guerrillas.

The Japs took both boys to the Casa. Manuelito insisted he was not Campos, he was Manuelito. The Japs rounded up the whole Escano family, Don Lorenzo, Don Augustine, Fermin, Johnny, Nonita, everybody they could find. They asked Manuelito to step up to each one in turn. Every time he stepped forward, they'd hit him in the face to knock him down. Then they'd kick him in the groin or stomach or head and pull him to his feet and say to his relative, "Is this Captain Campos?" They'd pull his bloody face back by the hair and thrust it into the face of the relative and say, "Is this Captain Campos?"

"It is our Manuelito."

"So sorry."

Then they would start again, going all the way down the line that way, through the large family and their in-laws and cousins, beating him before each one in turn, reviving him when he became unconscious and beating him unconscious again.

Manuelito was a whimpering rag of a man by the time he got to the end of the line. It was a beating from which he never recovered.

At the time of the original landing, Loling had taken her baby and fled to the hills with her husband Teting. But she could not stand the hill life. Her baby was sickly and she could not stand submitting it to the hardships there. She crept back into town at night and hid in the home of her uncle. After about three weeks, the Japs found her and took her to the Casa. They knew her husband was leader of the force holding the bridge north of the city.

People going by the Casa heard a girl's screams occasionally. The Jap commanding officer of southern Leyte and all his staff were staying at the Casa. Loling was very pretty.

Then all three Escanos disappeared from the Casa. We found out through Loling's muchacha. The muchacha was allowed to come every two or three days for Loling's laundry and to bring her fresh clothing. She did not see Loling. She just exchanged the clean bundle for the soiled one. After about a month, she was told she need not come any longer. Loling was not there.

Don Lorenzo called on the Jap commander to ask what had happened to his boys and to Loling. The commander said they had been shipped to Tacloban to be imprisoned there. Don Lorenzo went by Jap banca to Tacloban. It was difficult and required much bribery. It required more bribery to get a Jap officer to say they had no Escanos there, probably they were in Cebu. Then Don Lorenzo returned to Malitbog and, after more bribery, got passage to Cebu. No, no Escanos, perhaps Davao. After that Don Lorenzo gave up and returned to Malitbog to mourn his dead.

Then Fermin ran away to join the guerrillas in the hills. The Kempetai rounded up the whole Escano family again, and made a speech. If one more Escano male left Malitbog, they would butcher every male in the family. None would be spared, not the old nor the male infants.

Fermin was terrified for his wife after what happened to Loling. Fermin's wife had not wanted to leave with him for the hills. He promised he would return to rescue her from the city. He came back at night, took her past the guards, and got her by baroto to Hinundayan to the home of her parents.

His wife's father was in a rage. How dare you imperil my daughter and our family by these escapades, by joining the guerrillas, by sneaking my daughter past Jap guards? That was his attitude. His rage went on for hours. Fermin tried to shut it off by going to sleep. When he slept, his father-in-law stole his gun and brought it to the Japs.

"He is no more a guerrilla," he told them. "Here is what makes him a guerrilla," and he gave the Japs the gun.

The Japs made the old man responsible for Fermin. He had some kind of in with them that kept them from arresting Fermin. They did say if Fermin left Hinundayan, they would hold the old man.

Fermin could not make up his mind. The problem of wife, father-in-law, and the guerrillas was too entangled for him. He lingered over the untangling and the guerrillas darted into town and solved things for him. They grabbed him off and into the hills.

I don't know what happened to the old man, but Fermin became a scourge among guerrillas, fearlessly and steadily rampaging. He had to prove himself again to his boys, and he leaned over backwards to do it.

Finally, Curly came to me for safety. She was wearing the orange-red dress in which we had had our Christmas party. She was carrying all her belongings in a box about twice as big as a shoebox. She had been walking all night. She looked pitiful and like a kid that didn't know where to go or what to do.

"Oh, Richy," she said, "I am so afraid."

I put my arms around her. I remember I didn't kiss her, just put my arms around her and held her. I don't know why I didn't kiss her except I was so glad to see her it was enough just to hold her.

"You don't have to be afraid with me."

"There is so much death everywhere. I am so afraid."

"You've got the United States Navy to protect you here."

I found a family near by with whom she could stay, and thereafter we saw each other every day.

29

It was like a ship at sea there, my station in the jungle. I made a desk out of a door, and I had my radio receiver on it and a doorbell with a telegraph key to ring it. The doorbell was connected to the batteries. We charged the batteries at the same time we ran the engine to go on the air. I rang the bell to signal the engineer, just as if I were on the bridge of a ship. It saved shouting. One bell was to start, two to stop, three to reduce power, four to increase power, five to come in for chow. There was no signal to stop the engine. When it stopped, it was an accident. It took gasoline to start it, and gasoline was worth diamond-studded golden eyeteeth. We had plenty of crude oil. A Jap ship had been torpedoed off the coast and drums of oil had floated ashore. I had every civilian and every guerrilla for twenty miles down there three nights in a row grabbing the oil. But gasoline—Lord, oh Lord, oh gasoline!

Tuba distilling for fuel wasn't practical any more. The tuba grew down by the seacoast where the Japs were. The people wouldn't collect it. They were afraid the Japs would take it, and anyway we had nothing with which to make stills. The Japs had every truck and car everywhere.

But the "bridge" of the radio station and the evenings with Curly were about the only nice, non-snafu things I can remember. Curly came over every evening to help with chow, and after chow we would sit out in the jungle together. We were on the crest of the hills. There were no mosquitoes that high. We had cleared away some brush to give us a lookout for Jap ships on Sogod Bay, and Curly and I would sit watching the bay.

I remember mostly the nights when there was moonlight. The air was sweet and cool. There was a plant smell to it. The moon would make the leaves of the trees shiny, and the rays of the moon would come down through the trees in long thin columns like through church windows. There was a silvery swarming of moonbeams in the columns, and the hilltops would be frosted over with a mist of clouds. Sometimes we watched them until very late at night when the mist settled down into dew for the earth, and then we could look past the hills through a night so clear that it made you feel you were looking through to the end of forever.

There were plenty of jungle sounds to keep us company. Every hour on the hour and every half hour on the half hour, as regularly as if they had clocks in them, the Kalow birds would start up their kalow-kalow, kalaw-kalaw. One would start, to give the key sort of, and then all would join in from wherever they were for about fifteen seconds and all would shut off at the same time. It was as good as a cuckoo clock, only not so strident, not so peeping sort of, but deeper and more rumbling and you could hear the sound of the jungle clocks kalowing-kalowing over the hills and down towards the sea and down the other way for as far as your ears would carry. Then silence. This kept up until ten o'clock usually, sometimes only until nine, but as long as it lasted you could mark the half hours by it. It made the half hours seem to be friends walking out of your life, as if each half hour had to get up and leave when the Kalow bird kalowed.

There were owls. They have a very plaintive hoot in the Philippines. It is low and so sad like a mother regretting her child's little sorrow. The sound carries long distances and you can't tell whether it's coming from near or far because it permeates the air. You can't even make out the direction from which it came. It just comes into your ears from all over. There were white cockatoos with their squawking, shrewish screams at everything that disturbed them, even their own dreams. They'd just sit and scream themselves purple at their dreams. There was the bojong bird. During the mating season, the deer barked, real dog barks but the kind you hear when a dog has been hit and has run away and wants to come back but is afraid it will get hit again if it does, and sometimes Curly and I would become silent and hold ourselves real still and we could hear the jungle's night-flying insects, something like dragonflies, swishing and flitting with a little rapidly fluttering swoosh.

Then I'd walk Curly home. She always wanted to hear a story at the end. I'd tell her one about my childhood in Colorado or about my grandfather's cattle ranch.

"And now how about 'Jack and the Beanstalk'?" I'd say.

"Oh, that's first grade."

"How about a good, fast cowboy and Injun story?"

"Oh, I saw that in the movies."

Curly's best stories were about people, short, telling little anecdotes that sounded so compelling in her mouth. She was one of sixteen children, and her mother was one of sixteen. She had hundreds of relatives from first cousins on up, and each seemed to have a special amusing foible that Curly knew and would delight to tell. Her family had big carnivals back home. They'd dress up in domino costumes with full masks. The girls were very clever at it, said Curly, the boys not so clever. The girls acted naughty and could say naughty things because no one could be sure who was who. Once Curly danced seductively with her brother, Ed. After all, an older brother never pays much attention to his sister. Ed wanted a date right away. "Oh, sir," simpered Curly, "you flatter me, sir, you despise me, sir." She simpered in cheap Filipino, and Ed became more clamorous to escort her home. The next morning when the whole family was at breakfast, Curly broke out suddenly in the same simper, "Oh, sir, I am ashamed, sir, you flatter me, sir, you despise me, sir." Ed turned pink to the ears.

Curly began to cry after she told me this story.

"Why are you crying?" I asked, surprised.

"His ears," she sobbed, "stuck out like two little cute tiny pink elephants."

Curly had told the story so charmingly I had forgotten about Ed being killed by the Japs.

We used to talk about the great fiesta Don Lorenzo gave in 1943 to celebrate the birthday of Santa Maria, Malitbog's patron saint. It lasted a week. For the first night there was a costume dance with everybody dressed as pirates. The dance floor was 140 feet long and about 40 feet wide, and there were nice, soft electric lights with coconut oil as fuel for the Diesel-engined generator. The second night there was a Spanish operetta with local talent. Then another dance, and the selection of a queen of the fiesta with a real crown. Finally came Saturday, the big day. There was a lottery with a first prize of two thousand pesos. Little numbered balls were put in a big fine mahogany cylinder. Twenty balls rolled out one by one into a glass maze and wandered around until each had dropped into a separately numbered basket. The baskets were numbered according to the fighting cocks they had, the balls according to the lottery tickets. If your ticket drew a cock you were in the running for the big money.

The twenty cocks fought a free-for-all. They let them go in the pit all at one time. It was terrific. One cock licked seven in a row. The eighth one was a cock that had done no fighting at all. The cock that had licked seven was all tuckered out by that time so he lost to that yellow chicken of a cock that hadn't done a damn thing all night. The two thousand pesos went to the one who held a ticket on the cock that won the free-for-all, but there was a prize for everybody who drew a cock.

In the middle of the fiesta, about midnight, when the dancing was beginning to run down, Tom Jurika wandered off and listened to the midnight news on the big Scott radio. They announced the unconditional surrender of Italy. Tom went right back to the dance. He walked through the dancers to Major Francesco, so silently and looking so military that the dancers stopped slowly. It was like a scene in a movie. Tom ground to a halt before the major.

"Major," he said, in a loud, firm voice, "Italy has surrendered to us unconditionally."

"What is it? What is it?" It was Don Lorenzo pushing impatiently through the cheering crowd.

The old man was very proud of his radio. He listened to the news broadcasts twice a day. He let nothing ever interfere with that. He liked to be the first to relate the world's important happenings, and now here it was, the most important event since Pearl Harbor, and Tom had heard it first, over the old man's radio, too.

Irritability was the old man's first reaction to the news. Then he danced. For the first time since his wedding, more than thirty years before, he danced, and he danced all night, too. Everybody danced all night. The dance had been just about over when the news came, but everybody danced until long past dawn—and even the chaperons found swains to distract their giggling selves from their duties.

Oh, Curly and I must have gone to that fiesta a hundred times in our minds during the winter and spring of 1944. It was the only formal party we had ever gone to together in the way a girl and her fellow do when they have a date.

But as for the rest, if it wasn't one thing, it was another, and the whole business was just one damn thing after the other. I sent a radio set up to North Leyte with Capilius. We built it out of spare receivers, and out of this and that, and it took forever to get it working. Then it took three weeks for Capilius to walk the 120 kilometers to the new station. There were a lot of Japs around and he had to be cautious. Finally he went on the air. The transmitter worked, but the receiver wouldn't receive. It had worked all right for us, but it didn't for him and he didn't know how to fix it. I didn't have a man to spare to send to him. We were getting him all right, but he couldn't receive our messages saying we were hearing him fine and all he sent were plaintive queries, asking if we heard him.

I sent a runner up giving him a schedule, telling him to broadcast at eight in the morning and four in the afternoon. It took three weeks for the runner to get up there and three weeks to come back. The runner came back saying Capilius didn't have a watch and couldn't get one, short of killing a Jap. But he had no soldiers with him to kill a Jap. I sent the runner back with a watch, six weeks more for the round trip. Then the Jap patrols became most active at eight A.M. and four P.M. He couldn't broadcast at those times. He had to lay low. He asked for another schedule. I had to send another runner with it, six weeks more. After that, his watch became erratic. It was a pretty good watch. I had paid 125 pesos for it, but he didn't have a receiver to synchronize it with ours. It happened at a time when our fuel was short. We couldn't afford to keep our own receiver running indefinitely. There was no point sending a runner to synchronize watches. In six weeks, what couldn't happen to a watch in the humid jungle air? So all I could do was keep our receiver running for five minutes on the morning schedule and five minutes on the evening schedule and hope to hell we would hear from him.

There were no spare parts. When, for a change, I was going good, Mindanao would go off the air. The Japs came in there once with fifteen thousand men and a hundred airplanes and knocked hell out of Fertig's installations. It was a rabbit hunt all over hellangone, and Mindanao couldn't let a peep out of itself for more than two weeks.

Then the Japs would knock hell out of us. They came in on St. John's station. The first thing St. John knew, bullets were coming into the shack with him. He lifted himself sleepily on his elbows and wham! Perling Kuizon, who had been so handy around ordnance a year before but now since the capture of ordnance by the Japs had been helping in radio, landed on him and a tommy gun landed on him and he was knocked flat.

Kuizon had been sleeping in a little half loft in the shack. He had just rolled out the best he could with St. John's tommy gun when the bullets started hitting.

Johnny had prepared for just such an emergency. Each man had been assigned something to grab and run. But the kid assigned to grab the station's money—seventeen hundred pesos—pushed away the bag of pesos to take an extra pair of dirty old pants under it. He had been the only man in the station who had had two pairs of pants and he had been proud of that.

When Johnny got out of the hut, he saw about one hundred Japs—big guys, Koreans—coming down the hill towards him shooting. They didn't know what they were shooting at. They were just doing it to give themselves confidence or something. Johnny grabbed up his tommy gun, pulled the bolt back, and nothing happend. There was no clip. He ran back into the house, but he couldn't find it there. Probably it had fallen through the bamboo flooring. Then a bullet clipped the hair of him. Johnny had plenty of hair hanging down pretty long, and the bullet zipped through like a lighted match. He threw down his gun to give himself no encumbrances, put down his head, and ran.

But he thought only of running from Japs so he ran in the wrong direction. About fifty feet from the house, a field of Kogan grass began—high, very cutting grass. St. John knew he couldn't run through that. He'd leave a wake the Japs would shoot to pieces. A fallen tree lay out on the edge of the grass. St. John threw himself under that. There was a narrow space under there, enough for Johnny's skinny body, and the grass where Johnny had had to wade to get to the tree was wiry enough to snap back into place without leaving a trail. Johnny had a Smith and Wesson pistol which I had lent him. He cocked it. "Rich," he told me, "you could have heard the click of that hammer in China; I kept it oiled and everything, but the hammer just r'ared back roaring, saying, 'Here, old Jappies, here's Johnny, come and get him.' "

The Japs came over, swishing their bayonets from side to side, pushing the grass apart. A Jap walked along Johnny's tree, poking along the side of it. Johnny just lay still. He closed his eyes. He says his eyes felt so hot he thought they might look like signal lights.

A fall of rain came on. It hit on the log and dripped down on him. He didn't move. The red ants came out to work over the mud. They walked all over him. They walked on his eyelids and in his ears and looked up his nose. He didn't brush them off. He didn't dare move. He didn't move for five and one half hours. Every two or three minutes the Japs would fire shots indiscriminately into the jungle and grass and hills, just to keep the guerrillas away. Then they went away, taking everything Johnny had, including one hundred and fifty eggs, a sack of rice, the seventeen hundred pesos, and Johnny's shoes that I had brought him from the submarine.

The transmitter was lost, too. The kid who had grabbed it up found he couldn't run with it fast enough, so he just cracked it down against a log to make sure the Japs would get no use out of it and then took off.

No, there was no end to it, resistors burning out and transformers and tubes going and fellows losing their nerve and saying they had to evacuate their families to safety, then not coming back and guards telling me they didn't have to work, but just guard . . . well, they God-damn well had to work if they were around my camp, everybody had to work. And politics! My, yes, there certainly was politics. Certain officers had the idea that if they made the guerrilla movement all-Filipino and manip-ulated the Americans out of it, it would look better in the history books. It would confront MacArthur and the United States with the fact that the Filipinos had had a major share in their own liberation—or something like that. The intrigues and manipulations that went on made you think you were sitting in with the courts of Europe on the Congress of Vienna instead of a hole-in-the-pants, banana-for-dinner army that had nothing to fight with except naked heart. Some Americans didn't help things along very much by just saying the hell with it and going off to sit out the war, taking with them a girl and pesos, neither of which belonged to them.

But to make a very long, very exasperating, very boring, very frustrating story short: Leyte never went altogether off the air. Somebody always passed a miracle and kept us going by hook or by crook or by the devil knows what all. It wasn't me that did it. It was all of us together, each coming up somehow with the brass ring, and I think we were the only island that never lost contact with MacArthur for a single day no matter what happened.

Then our submarine came in, and after that it was beautiful.

30

When the submarine came in, I thought my mission would be over and I would be recalled to Souwespac. I had trained enough Filipino personnel to run all the radio equipment they could possibly send up. I said good-by to Curly. It was very hard to do.

"I am not sure," I said, "but I think there will be orders for me on the submarine."

She walked with me a ways.

"I feel such pain," I said, "as if my life were ending."

"It is only an intermission in the play."

"But the pain of the intermission is so great, it's as if it was an ending."

"Maybe, darling, the orders will be to stay."

"Maybe."

"Then we will be so happy."

"I will engrave the orders in gold and hang them on the wall of our house—if we ever have a house, if we ever have the orders."

"The miracle will happen. We are not ordinary people. We do not live ordinary. Ordinary things, like partings, do not happen to us."

"Maybe," I said.

I gave her everything I had except 10 pesos. I gave her all my cigarettes because they were valuable for barter—10 to 20 pesos a pack. But I found later she had slipped a whole carton back into my pack. I had a big ball of thread, thousands of yards. I gave that to her. Thread was very valuable. Abacá fiber won't fit in a sewing machine and the people there unravel old shirts and rags

198

to get thread. I gave her my watch, worth about 120 pesos. I gave her eight pairs of wool socks I had got off the Japs. Those could be unraveled, too, and the wool rolled into balls and sold.

We had to have another miracle to bring the sub in. A condenser on the radio set broke down. Then the batteries started to go. We hooked two batteries together by stripping and taping to get enough voltage to send a message. It was the last message those batteries sent. Then they crapped out altogether. But the last one did the trick. It completed the arrangements for the sub.

A U. S. submarine broke water off our beach about six o'clock at night. We had four thousand Filipinos waiting to unload it. There was no pier. It had to be unloaded with barotos. We had fifty of them, but we had to lash them in pairs to give a platform to hold anything. The skipper kept the sub trimmed down by pumping ballast so that we could throw the cargo over the side.

"Where are the Japs?" he asked.

"They are five kilometers below us and seven kilometers above us," I told him.

"My boy," he said, "if you are trying to scare us, you are doing a good job."

The Japs did send a patrol up to find out what all the noise was about. But one hundred and fifty guerrillas were waiting for them in trenches they had dug with their bolos, and the Japs that got out of that, got out running.

Then the Japs sent ships. Three came bouncing, their guns pointing. But there was nothing for them to shoot at. The sub had gone and we had gone, carrying more guns than Kangleon had soldiers for, more radios—brand-new, wonderful, glistening, powerful, United States Navy radios—than we had operators for, and medical equipment, big medical chests. I remember Doc Parado opened one of them up on the beach. Then he just sat looking.

"Now I have to read my books again to remember what all this is for," he said when I came up. There were tears of happiness in his eyes. He felt like a doctor again, and I noticed that suddenly a bedside manner had come back to him.

However, there were no orders for me to leave. Instead there were two Americans on board whom I was instructed to assist in setting up a weather station—Sgt. Hank Chambliss, a big-handed, dark, powerful-looking, 190-pound football player from Georgia, and Corporal Gamertsfelder from Athens, Ohio, I think, whose father is president of Ohio University. Gamertsfelder is the kind of fellow who can make friends with anybody. He is very serious, then he busts out with a smile and you think how nice he is. Chambliss didn't talk very much. I never got to know him well. I didn't have time, as it turned out. All I know about him was that he knew his job and was a hard, conscientious worker.

The boys were very nervous at first. I had a fine time acting the veteran for them. "Oh, we've got nothing to worry about; there ain't a Jap nearer than a hundred yards of here," that sort of thing. They had four tons of equipment with them, and I rounded up sixty Filipino boys to carry for us. Then we struck back for my place—and Curly.

In the end, I was so anxious to see Curly that I went the last two miles alone. We had been hiking for three days and I was dirty. There was mud up past my behind from slipping on the trails. My jungle boots were in half. The rubber bottoms hold out fine in the jungle, but the sand gets into the seams separating the rubber from the canvas top and rubs them away and mud comes in and fungus grows in the mud and sand and starts eating the canvas. After that the leeches come through. I had leeches all over me when I saw Curly. I hadn't stopped to pull them off.

But it didn't last long. As soon as the weather station was established, a message came that I was to go to southern Samar, establish a radio station, and plot a mine field at Surigao Straits between Homonhon and southern Leyte.

I knew what that meant. MacArthur was on his way.

I didn't tell Curly about it. I just waited until the last minute. Then I said good-by. I felt so strange walking away from her. The drama of the Philippines was coming to its climax, this tremendous thing, and here I was walking down a stubbly, littered, very quiet jungle path, feeling sorrow in me and a sense of strangeness.

31

Homonhon Island is less than six miles long and a mile and a half wide at its widest point. Jap patrols came to it every now and then. Jap ships passed daily. Suluan Island, four miles away in the Surigao Straits, was garrisoned by Jap marines. And there was no place really to hide on Homonhon from a determined search. I had only six soldiers with me to beat off a search, so run it would have to be and on a place like Homonhon you could run only until your hat floated.

The local population gathered to watch us land. We were a fairly respectable-looking party in comparison with what we would have been before the sub. We had two transmitters—a large one and a walky-talky. We had a gun for every man and cartridges for every gun. We had medicines and *I Shall Return—MacArthur* magazines and soap and chocolate and matches, all marked *"I Shall Return—MacArthur."* I handed them out among the people. There were 1944 pictures in the magazines. They proved to the people we were in touch with MacArthur. There were pictures of pin-up girls in the magazines. The Homonhonos rolled their eyes over that. The women looked contemplative and pensive when they saw the pin-up girls. But the pictures of Japanese sinkings caught their hearts and the nice, big, easy-to-understand maps showing what Nimitz and MacArthur had done thus far caught their minds. I had aspirin for the people and quinine and Atabrine—the island was crowded with malaria— and I told them MacArthur had sent this for them to show how he always thought of the people of the Philippines. Then I asked them to come at six-thirty in the evening, I would tune in San Francisco for them and get the news broadcast by the Office of War Information in Visayan—the native dialect.

Then I made a "Victory is not far off" speech and an "I will return—MacArthur" speech. I knew how the people felt. A certain proportion of them, being true Filipinos, would want liberty at any price. MacArthur talk would put ferocity into them. A larger proportion would want peace at any price. MacArthur talk would get them on the bandwagon. They would realize that was the price of peace.

Oh, I felt quite the clever young man, I tell you, and as a grand finale I ordered that no banca could put out from the island for any reason without our written permission. I knew the people would warn me of any banca that slipped away during the night and give us time to run until our hats floated.

"One must be killed," said Alibongbong, one of my boys. "It will be an example, and then he is a proved fifth columnist."

"No, no killing here, not until he does something against us."

"He has done something already. He is a fifth columnist."

"He hasn't done anything against us."

"That is against us, to be a fifth columnist."

"Well," I said, "bring him to me."

The fifth columnist arrived with his very pretty young daughter. He brought her to help touch my heart, and it did. It touched my heart that a father should bring his daughter on such an errand. He was a man about forty-five, wiry and nervous and small, a former politico of some wealth and material substance. He had buqweed to Homonhon with his family from Samar because the guerrillas there had wanted to execute him.

"Why?"

He had a long, familiar story to tell about Japanese pressure on him.

"I helped as little as possible," he said. "I ran away as soon as I could."

I knew he had run away only when the guerrillas had become so strong they were capable of putting into effect their threat to execute him.

Then Captain Valley had come to Homonhon from Samar to hide from the Japs until their search for him could dwindle. The Japs came in a launch. The fifth columnist had guided them about Homonhon during their unsuccessful search there for Captain Valley.

"Why?"

"It was to save my son's life. A father cannot be expected to do less."

I did not say anything. Local people had come into the house to witness the questioning. There were thirty or forty of them. They all remained very silent. They did not seem to be either for or against the fifth columnist. They seemed to concentrate on watching me.

"I was fishing when the Japs arrived. I ran. They caught my son on the beach. I was afraid they would kill him if I did not return."

The story took a long time to tell. I felt the man could have said what he had to say in a short time if he were innocent. But the people around him showed no emotion. They did not protest any part of his story. They remained silent and inscrutable, and watching me.

"Your life is in our hands," I said at last. "We will preserve it."

Alibongbong made a move towards me. I looked at him angrily and frowned him into motionlessness. It was very complicated there. I believed the people were silent because they felt the fifth columnist had Jap influence, and they were still afraid of the Japs. If we killed this man, we would force the people to take a stand—either for the man or against him. Some might resent being forced. A few might become so afraid of remaining silent in the face of the death of a Jap ally that they would go to the Japs to absolve themselves of the deed. If we did not kill this man, then the people could feel perhaps we did not intend to stay. Eventually, we would leave without having done anything to bring the wrath of the Japs upon their heads.

"But any suspicious action upon your part," I concluded, "will finish you. You will be brought to trial, if not before me, then before other guerrillas, if not before other guerrillas, then before your liberated people when MacArthur returns. There will be no escape for you anywhere."

"Oh, sir, you may rely on me."

"I do not rely on anything in you except your fear of death."

Alibongbong scowled at me. Then he prodded the man from the room with his gun.

The big new radio did not work. We tried for four days, taking it apart and putting it together, taking it apart again and putting it together again, shifting from location to location to location. Then it occurred to me how stunted and twisted up the trees of Homonhon were, and how red the earth was. The island was just one big block of iron. We put the baby set on the banca, hoisted the antenna on the mast, took the banca out about twenty feet from shore and grounded the set in the water. It worked fine.

But it was late August then. Wind came first from the northeast, then from the southwest, and sometimes both winds blew together. It made the water choppy, and choppy water was too dangerous for delicate radio equipment. I found a lee behind a point, but the jut of land blanked out the radio. We just had to go along on the basis of God willing.

It did not take long to plot the channels through the mine fields. Jap ships of all sizes passed frequently. I had an alarm clock with me and a small army compass with a pelorus arrangement.

"Destroyer, distance 1600 yards, time 1028 hours, bearing 090, course 275, speed twenty-five knots." I'd rap that out and Reposar would mark it down. Distance, course, bearing, and speed were taken every minute until the ship was out of sight. The figures cross-checked against each other. The compass enabled me to be accurate about the course and bearing. I could check my estimates on distance and speed against them.

I used to sit in a house right on the beach, just a little bit back from my window with my binoculars to my eyes. The ships came very close. I could make out the expressions on the Jap faces there sometimes, and could get the whole feel of just what it was like on those ships. It was fun.

Then one morning when Reposar was in the banca trying to make contact, I heard a swishing up above and there was a float Zero coasting directly over us at about 150 feet. I could see the pilot in the plane. He was looking at the banca with binoculars. Reposar was lying down, working the set, with earphones to his head. When he heard the swish, he pulled one earphone off and looked up. He ran for the mast and frantically yanked down the antenna. He got it down while the Jap plane was still there. Then Reposar began screaming for a baroto to get him ashore. He thought the plane would come back to strafe.

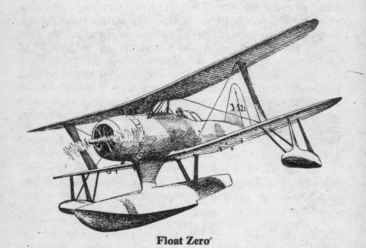

Float Zero

The plane didn't come back, but about four o'clock that afternoon a Jap destroyer escort came nosing along the coast at four knots. I got all the equipment out of our house and hidden, and I deployed my men in the high grass just off the beach. There was no point running and we could kill some, anyway, of those who landed. But nobody landed. The destroyer escort just nosed along at four knots, the bow and bridge and starboard side full of men peering with binoculars, and then finally nosed out of sight. I guess the airplane hadn't been able to give them a very accurate fix on our position.

We made one haul on that island—a floating mine.

We towed it ashore by baroto. I told the boys to leave it alone until I could help them with it—I had messages to get out—but Alibongbong was too curious. He got hold of a piece of pipe for a hammer and a leaf of an auto spring for a chisel. Then he hammered off the access plate and reached inside and took out the booster charge and primer. He came holding these things. If I had known what he had been up to, I'd have been building the biggest foxhole man ever did see, instead of just sitting calmly writing messages. I knew about such things from my service on a mine sweeper.

But Alibongbong said he knew about such things, too, from having been a fisherman. He had fished with mine powder before. We gave the powder to the fishermen of Homonhon. They had dynamite caps—but no dynamite—and short fuses. They mixed the powder with water and let it dry out into blocks. They then wrapped the blocks of powder in layer after layer of rattan and put in a stone to weight it. When they went fishing, they took along a *cayo*—a piece of coconut husk which holds a spark indefinitely. When you need fire, you just blow on the *cayo*. One man would search for fish under the coral. When he found a quantity of them, they'd light the fuse and lower the dynamite cautiously to the coral. Then they'd paddle like hell to get away from the explosion. It took a nice touch on the paddle. Ripples would have scared the fish. Then boom, and knocked-out fish floating to the surface. Then everybody would paddle like hell to grab the fish because as soon as the fish recovered consciousness they'd wobble off.

I took the whole mine apart to get the electrical wire and the circuits. I have a passion for spare parts, so great by this time that I don't think a lifetime of plenty could cure it any more.

When the channels through the mine fields were accurately plotted and dispatched to Souwespac, I split up my crew and took off with half of them for Samar. I figured those who remained on Homonhon would be reasonably safe without a white face around. If Japs came, they could just hide their guns and then nobody would be able to tell them from the rest of the population.

But the boys were still afraid of the fifth columnist.

As soon as I left, they brought him over to the radio station. They bought a chicken for him—30 centavos. Then they told him to cook it.

He cooked it outdoors. The people of the island began to gather around him.

"Eat it," commanded one of the guerrillas.

"All?"

"Yes."

"Will you have some with me, please? It is very tender."

"No, the whole chicken is for you."

"You are most generous, but I do not understand. What fiesta is there?"

"It is not a fiesta. It is a custom."

"I am sorry, but it puzzles me."

"It puzzles you because you have taken the culture of the *Hapons* for yours."

"No, I have nothing to do with the *Hapons*."

"Then you would understand that in our culture the condemned man is allowed to have whatever he wants for his last meal. We could not ask you what you wanted because we might not have it. Instead we give you the best we have."

The man put down the chicken.

"Eat it," commanded the guerrilla. He waved with his tommy gun.

"Surely you are not serious. I have the word of the American."

"He is not here. Eat the chicken, please."

"But the American said, it was a decree."

"This is not America. This is the Philippines. Eat the chicken. You said yourself it is very tender."

"It sticks in my throat. The American, you yourself heard him." He looked imploringly at the people around him. "You all heard him. You were there and are my witnesses."

The people remained silent.

"Eat the chicken," commanded the guerrilla and leveled his gun. "Lick the bones."

They forced him to take all the meat from the bones. Then the guerrilla said, "Walk off a little way, please," and said, "Now turn around," and fired. He aimed at the chest.

The first bullet hit the chest and then walked up into the neck and blew off the back of the man's head.

"Now," announced the guerrilla, "there is no one left to talk if the Japs come with sea water for us."

I heard about this too late to do anything but wring my hands.

32

I put out for Samar on an evening early in September. I
forget the exact date. I left the walky-talky set on Homonhon because they needed something there they could hide
in a hurry and took with me the big set. It was quite a
bundle—a barrel of fuel, a demijohn of lubricating oil, a
charger, four batteries, the receiver, the speaker, the transmitter, whatever spare parts I could find, plus our personal
gear and guns.

There was no wind and we had to scull. At midnight
when we were abreast of Manicani Island, the current
changed and set for Guyuan Island, three kilometers away,
where there was a large garrison of Japs. I put in to
Manicani. I sent a man wading ashore. He woke up a
native. The native said there weren't any Japs on the
island, and we found a nice anchorage on the southeast
coast and hove to there and went to sleep.

I didn't want to travel to Samar by day. We'd have to
pass too close to Guyuan and we'd have to use the Jap
launch route. I decided to wait for a favorable wind that
would carry us against the current at night. When daylight
came and we woke up, I had the radio brought ashore and
began to set it up to make contact with the master station
on Leyte and report whatever ships would pass.

While we were still working at it, a Filipino boy came
running up. He said four BCs had just landed from
Guyuan and were breakfasting at Manicani barrio.

"Who are you?" I asked.

"I was at Bataan, sir."

"What outfit?"

He told me.

"Who was on your left?"

He told me.

That was enough for me. There is a fraternity among men who fought on Bataan. It is impossible to believe that one who was there would let down anybody else who was there.

The guerrillas do not ordinarily bother BC (Bureau of Constabulary) garrisons. The BCs are Filipino police working for the Japs, but the Japs do not entrust them with mortars or heavy weapons. They do not kill fellow Filipinos the way the Japanese do. The most they do is burn houses and they do this only when circumstances force their hands. They require the people to remain in their homes in the garrison barrios so that they can live off them. In order to enforce this, they announce that they will loot the homes of all who buqwee and then burn them down. They do it. They carry out their threat. But the guerrillas do not bother the BC garrisons because they know that if they wipe out the BCs the Japs will replace them with their own troops and heavy weapons and mortars and policy of torture and slaughter.

However, this was different. We had to stay on the island until nightfall. Jap marines were only three kilometers away. They could see Manicani barrio from where they were. They could hear a signal shot fired from a rifle.

I left Pop with the radio set and took Teodoro and Donayre with me. I had a tommy gun for myself and another for one of the boys. The third had a carbine. Then we started out for Manicani barrio.

We had three and one-half kilometers to walk. The sun was very hot. There was no wind at all, and you could taste the heat of the air as you breathed it. We did not say anything. We all walked along until we came to a kind of water hole just outside the town. There was a woman bathing there. She started to run away, but I pointed my gun at her.

"I am sorry," I said, "you must stay with us awhile."

I couldn't take a chance on her alarming the BCs. She was a young, very pretty woman, shapely and firm-breasted. She wore a cotton dress. Filipinas bathe that way in public, in their dresses. Her dress had fallen below her breast on one side, but she was too fearful to notice. She stood with feet planted wide, looking at me imploringly and in terror.

"We shall not hurt you," I said. "We just want you to remain still. You may continue your bathing if you like."

She shook her head. She was still mute with fear. I told her to walk to where I would be between her and the town and remain there. Then I sent the boy who had warned us into town to locate the BCs and report back to me.

I remember how it was so quiet there the birds sounded extra loud and a dog running up the dusty road made distinct little puffy pattering sounds. The girl pulled her dress up over her breast, and adjusted her hair. Her fear was subsiding. She sat tranquilly. I kept thinking what bad luck this was. If only the BCs had not come in the morning. If only they had come in the evening or the next day. I didn't know then for whom the luck would be bad, but certainly it was true that, whichever way the luck went, it would be bad for someone—either the BCs or us.

It was a kind of a main path there out of town. People came drifting up in ones and twos to get water, and we held them. We would not let them go back. We could not risk someone warning the BCs. A child came, a little girl. In a little while, we could hear her mother calling.

"Instruct the child to remain quiet," I told Teodoro.

The mother called again and again. The child stood looking at us with large, troubled eyes. Then the mother came hurrying up the path. When she saw us, she stopped short. I motioned her towards us with my gun. She came hesitantly, then she rushed past me and snatched up her child.

"We are not going to hurt anyone," I said. "We just want you to stay awhile."

The jungle was not very thick along the path, and around the water hole there was a clearing. Eventually, we had nine or ten people gathered there. I kept smiling at them and laughing to ease their fear. There was an elderly man among them. He spoke English in a soft, very courtly voice.

"It is plain that someone will be killed this morning," he said.

"No," I shook my head. "We do not want to hurt

212

anyone. We just want to disarm some BCs and hold them until night when we leave."

"And if they decline?"

"That will be their doing."

"If they are stubborn?"

"That will be their fault."

"Then someone will be killed."

"It has happened that way. We cannot move by daylight. We cannot trust them to remain quiet with the Japs so near."

"It is too bad you do not remain hidden until night."

"Yes, but there may be fifth columnists on the island who will warn them we are here. We cannot trust that with the Japs so near."

"It is too bad, but you are right."

"It is not our doing. We are willing to remain quiet. We have no war with Filipinos, only with Japs."

"Justice is with you. There are fifth columnists who will warn the BCs."

"We do not like to kill Filipinos, only Japs."

"Justice is with you and God goes with justice," the old man said sadly in his soft voice.

Finally, our scout came back. It had taken him so long because he had gone home to change into his best white clothes, to wash and to comb his hair.

"Sir," he protested when I complained at the delay, "it is the first blow I strike since Bataan."

Just before coming to us, he had looked into the house by the beach where the BCs were staying while food was being prepared for them. He said two of them were sleeping, one of them was talking to a girl as she cooked, and a fourth was just sitting there. There were four Enfield rifles with them—one for each man.

There was a church directly opposite the house with the BCs. The church was about forty feet long by twenty feet wide and made of galvanized iron. The walls were of iron, the roof of iron. Only the cross was wooden. There was a small iron shed alongside in which three church bells were housed, and the big iron hammers to strike them. We went into the church. It was empty.

I told my boys we would do it this way. Teodoro would station himself to command the front entrance of

the house on the left of where I would be in the church. Donayre would station himself to command the back entrance, and I would remain in the church where I could spray both front and back exits with my tommy gun. The scout would go into the house unarmed and tell the BCs they were surrounded and ask them to come out with their hands holding their heads.

There was a whole row of little houses along the street. A family came hurriedly out of one of them. They had seen us. A man was carrying two small children, one on his back, the other in his arms. A woman was carrying a third child in her arms and shooing along some other children, pushing at them with her knees. We watched them nervously. They hurried up the street. They had sense enough not to make any noise and just hurried along and out of sight. We watched the house with the BCs a long time to make sure they had noticed nothing wrong. I heard the girl in there with them laugh and say something protesting. Her laugh sounded so dripping there in the bright, hot, bleached-looking, dazzling air, so laving and brushing and seductive, so like a laugh in a bed. Then a man cried out something in Visayan.

"What did he say?" I asked Donayre.

"He said, 'How can she cook when you keep feeling her all the time? Has your stomach fallen into your balls?'"

Then the scout said he thought it would be better if he stood outside the hut and called to the BCs to surrender. Otherwise they might hold him as a hostage and

Enfield Model 1917

perhaps try to come out with his body as a screen.

"Will you call in Visayan or in English?"

"Sir, Visayan only."

"I do not understand Visayan."

"Sir, one speaks English, the sergeant. But I do not know about the others, sir. They may not only."

"You must be very careful what you say."

"Sir, I was at Bataan, sir."

"Yes, but I am very serious and you must be very careful what you say to them."

"Sir, yes."

"Because I am very serious and the eye of my gun will be watching you all the time."

"Sir, I fought at Bataan. I would fight with the guerrilla, but there is none on the island."

"All right, but I am very serious."

"Sir, yes."

He saluted the major's oak leaf that Curly had darned into my shirt with yellow thread.

"What will you tell them?" I asked.

"Sir, that they are surrounded, that if they do not wish to die, they must come out with their hands holding their heads, with their guns left behind. If they run, sir, they will be killed. They must not run or do anything to get killed."

He spoke in a very low tone. We all spoke very low. We were quite close to the house with the BCs.

"Well, that's right," I said, "but you must remember my gun will be on you and I am very serious and I do not understand Visayan well, just words here and there."

"Sir, I was at Bataan until the end."

"Well, yes," I said, "I was at Bataan, too, but today I am very serious."

Then Teodoro and Donayre took up their positions. I went to a window of the church, just an opening it was, really, and drew a bead on the house. Then this Filipino boy with his white clothes shining so hard it hurt to look at him went out of the church and over towards the house and began shouting towards the door.

The sergeant in command came out immediately. He began walking towards the church, curious, his hands down. When he saw me, he threw his hands up behind his head and clasped them and shouted to the others to come out unarmed. He shouted in Visayan, but I could follow what he was saying. The others did not come out. There was only silence from the house.

Then there was a shot from Teodoro and I could see under the house that there were feet running. The house was up on stilts and there were chickens under it, lying there out of the sun. People in the Philippine barrios and hills generally keep chickens under their houses on account of the snakes. The snakes like to come into the houses where it's cooler by day and warmer by night, but if they see chickens they will go for them first. Then you have warning of the snake from the squawks of the chickens. I could see through the chickens to where the feet were running and at the shot from Teodoro the man dropped prone into my sight and lifted his rifle and lowered his face towards the barrel. I opened up on him. I shot under the house through the chickens. A chicken blew backwards and another blew straight up into the air, smacking against the house, and the man bounced into the air and flopped backwards and flopped again and then lay still while chickens with necks stretched ran in all directions and people started running from their houses, climbing out of windows and jumping from doors and running up and down the street and away out of sight, and the sergeant started blowing his whistle. I turned my gun on the sergeant. He took his whistle out of his mouth and lifted it high into the air and slammed it against the ground.

"The whistle is to surrender," he screamed and ran a few steps towards me.

"Put your hands behind your head," I said. I spoke very calmly. I remember how surprised I was to hear the calmness in my voice.

The sergeant stopped short, and clasped his hands behind his head.

Then Teodoro and Donayre came out into the open. They were holding their rifles. The two remaining BCs stood between them with their hands in the air.

"Keep an eye on the sergeant," I told them and ran down to the back of the church and out of it. Our scout was frisking the men. He found a toy pistol on the sergeant. It was just an ordinary 49-cent cap pistol that the Japs had given him to pull a bluff in an emergency if he was caught without his rifle.

"Why do you murder?" cried the sergeant. "We surrender."

"Why did your man run? Why did your man jump out the window on the other side?"

"You shouldn't shoot."

"I didn't want to shoot. They made me."

"You shoot, you murder, you just want to shoot."

I ran over to him and put my gun against his chest. I was crazy there for a minute. My finger itched crazily against the trigger.

"They ran," I screamed. "You son of a bitch, they ran. They made me."

Then I went over to the other side of the house where the man I had shot lay. The sergeant ran along with me. The man was quite young. He had large brown eyes. He was pulling feebly at his throat and gasping for air.

He had been hit in the neck. I had hit right where I was shooting. I had fired seventeen rounds in three bursts. I got him on the first burst and then I had thrown a burst to the left of him and another to the right of him in case anybody else was running there that I couldn't see on account of the chickens. Only one bullet of the burst had gone into him because tommy guns tend to lift, but the bullet had torn out his whole throat and punctured his spinal column.

"You shouldn't have run," I said.

I had a morphine syrette from our medicine chest and put it into him.

"Why did you run," cried the sergeant, "when your orders were from me to surrender?"

The boy looked at me and then he looked at the sergeant. He opened his mouth to say something, but nothing came out except a terrible sound, like a dragging sort of whistling. Then he closed his eyes and after a moment or so became quiet.

I thought maybe the morphine was taking effect, but he was dead.

"I told him to surrender," said the sergeant. "He should not have run."

33

"What is your signal to the Japs?" I asked the sergeant.

I knew the Japanese marines at Guyuan must have heard the shooting.

"We have none. We expected nothing."

"I must be very sure."

"You can be sure."

"I will keep a watch on Guyuan. If we see a boat putting out, we shall shoot you."

"Shoot, shoot," he cried. "You can be sure we had no signal. We expected nothing here. It was just routine to come here."

"And if you do not return by evening?"

"They do not expect us until tomorrow."

"And what of the shooting here? They must have heard it."

"What do they care? They will expect that we have taken care of it. The Japanese do not rush towards shooting unless they must."

"Yes," I agreed, "that's sensible to believe."

We were standing talking by the body. I did not know what to do with the prisoners we had taken. It had not occurred to me we would take any prisoners. Then the girl they had been playing with rushed out of the house. She had been cowering in hiding all this time. She ran with head down straight past us and towards the jungle. She was not very pretty and she was a little fat, and the soft parts of her jiggled up and down as she ran, but she ran in great terror.

"Love has wings," grinned Teodoro.

"Are you the one whose stomach fell into his balls?" asked Donayre politely.

"No," replied the sergeant. "It was he who is dead. He had too much wires in him from love. That was why he ran."

I told the BCs they could come with us and be part of our organization if they gave their word they would not try to escape. The sergeant and one of the others agreed at once. The third man said he preferred to return to his wife in Guyuan.

"I would prefer to sit in the palace at Tokyo and write the peace," I cried, "and have geisha girls to fill my inkwell."

"He means," explained Teodoro, "he will shoot you if you do not agree."

"Oh, then, I agree. I promise."

We had to bury the dead one ourselves. All the people of the town had buqweed except a woman next door to the house that had held the BCs. She had had a baby that morning. Even her husband had buqweed. Only she and her baby remained.

We buried the boy in the churchyard. Teodoro took the boy's uniform—a sort of grayish purple outfit with short pants and a short-sleeved shirt, both in the same color. It was too new for him to resist.

"Now you look like a Goddamn BC," I told him.

"Oh, sir, no." He grinned happily. "Not with my honest face."

The only thing that distinguished him from a BC was the tommy gun. But his dress was not unusual among guerrillas. Whenever our soldiers killed a Jap, they would appear in complete Jap uniform. Five days before Mac-Arthur landed, Colonel Kangleon ordered his soldiers to remove all Jap uniforms, but most refused. A Jap uniform is a badge of honor. You cannot disrobe a Jap until you have killed him. The guerrillas were very puzzled when American soldiers shot at them in their Japanese uniforms. "We have not Japanese faces," they cried. Neither have many Japs, they were told, and then they took off their uniforms and put them away to wear after the war.

34

September 12 Admiral Halsey's planes came. By that time I had set my radio station up in southern Samar near Balangigi and the transmitter had broken down. We had fixed it and the generator had broken down. We fixed the generator and it broke down again and burned all the way out and we stole some generators out of the automobiles in the BC garrison barrio. Then we had to go back and steal the fan belts. We had a lot of trouble breaking into where the first car was. Then that didn't have a fan belt. We had to break into where a second car was.

I tell you all this to show you the frame of mind we were in when the planes finally came. I was in trouble with Major Charlie Smith about the BCs I had captured. He wanted to know what the hell I was doing with the enemy in my camp. I said they were good boys, living up to their promise to co-operate with us, and I was starving for help. He said to get them up to his prison on the double and I said, "Major Richardson to Major Smith: I'm sorry, pal, but okay." Coming up to southern Samar, I had gambled on finding a radio operator rather than taking one with me from Leyte. The only radio operator in the whole area was a fifth columnist. I put him to work. The only radio mechanic in the area was being held in a concentration camp by the guerrillas. They let him out for me and I put him to work, too. He had had fifteen years' experience working around mining operations. When Charlie heard about my campful of spies, he went so far up into the air it took five strong guerrillas to get him down again.

"Major Richardson to Major Smith: I do not care about politics. I just want this station running. If the only way to get on the air is to use Japanese with a bayonet up their butt, I will do that. I do not have a bayonet, but I will grind down a bolo to fit and get on the air. Repeat. On the air."

Then a Jap patrol of fifty came looking for me and I had to move. They came looking for me again and I had to move again. They found a civilian and bayoneted him in the abdomen. He ran five kilometers before dropping. Word got back to me. I had a medicine chest and a book called *Miracles of Modern Medicine* and some old *Reader's Digests* with medical articles in them that I had read, and it was up to me to show the local population we were out to do them some good. The Japs were going to be rough with the people on my account, and it was up to me to offset that the best I could, so I sent for the boy.

"He is dying," they told me.

"Then I can't do him any harm. Bring him."

He was brought on a homemade litter. He had run without trying to hold his guts in, just blind afraid running, and when I saw him he looked dead. His intestines were all the way out. There were flies over them and his face had that color of bleached shiny wood that the faces of the dead have. The book said not to take sulfadiazine when hit in the belly, but the intestines were not punctured. I looked them over carefully. There wasn't a scratch on them, just this hole about an inch long in the wall of the abdomen, and with the flies and all I was sure he would get peritonitis unless something was done, so I turned the page on the book that said not to take sulfadiazine and gave him a bunch of the stuff. The color came back to him and he became conscious.

I tell you, when I saw that boy with all the stuff hanging out through the wall of the abdomen, my heart sank. I hadn't figured on anything like that. The book was no help there. It said how to give pills and how to shake down a thermometer and put the head down and put the head up and hold your breath while listening for the heartbeat, but nothing about anything like this. However, I was the only one there who could even read the book, so it was up to me all right, plain enough, no ducking that.

"You can't live with that sticking out," I said to the

boy. I remembered reading somewhere where you can't operate without consent of the patient or someone authorized to act for him.

The boy closed his eyes.

"It is plain," said one of the men who had brought him. "No one has seen a man to live like that."

"I don't know a thing about how to put the intestines back or even where they belong. But they don't belong out like that. Everybody knows as much as that, and he will certainly die if they are out."

"He will certainly die."

"So if he's willing, I'm willing to try the best I can to get them back in."

"How can he not be willing?"

"Ask him. Some people might prefer to die in peace rather than be mauled around and made to pain before dying."

"No one prefers to die in peace. The drowning man grabs the straw. The falling man grabs the air."

"Ask him."

The man leaned over and said something to the boy in Visayan. The boy answered with eyes closed.

"He says he wishes for you the best of good wishes, sir."

I tried pushing the intestines in by hand. When I first started, I nearly fainted. But I put my head down and then I was all right for the rest of the time. My hands were trembling, but I forced them to their work and after a while they stopped trembling and my legs began to tremble. I didn't bother about them, though. It was just my hands and arms.

The intestines wouldn't go in. I couldn't figure out how so much of them had fallen through an opening not over an inch long, but I guess his running had stretched the muscles and worked them through. Then the gas had come and puffed them out like a bladder. After about fifteen minutes of pushing with my fingers, I took a razor blade and made the opening in his abdomen wall about a quarter of an inch longer. Donayre was helping me. He kept making powder out of the sulfadiazine tablets and I kept sprinkling the powder on. Then the stuff started to go back in. I spread the opening with my fingers and pushed with my thumb and they started to go back in. It took two hours altogether to get them in.

I got some abacá fiber, threaded it through a needle, twisted it to give it more strength, and then knotted it. I didn't know what kind of a stitch to use. It didn't say that in the book, either. It said plenty of other things in the book. It helped me a lot with a lot of patients, but for this boy the book was just a blank, and I had to write my own as I went along. I held my finger inside the cut as a sort of darning gourd to keep from sewing up the intestines. I couldn't push the needle through with my fingers. I had to use pliers, and while I was yanking with the pliers I noticed the boy looking at me. His eyes were full of horror.

"It feels better already," he said.

Donayre translated for me.

"There is pain now to tell me I am alive," the boy said.

"Tell him I have one more morphine syrette and he may have it if the pain is too great. But it is my last, I do not know where I will get another, and the pain must be actually very great."

"He says," translated Donayre, "he likes the pain to tell him he is alive."

I took seven stitches. For the last stitch I couldn't get my finger in any more, so I just grabbed hold of a bunch of skin near the opening and shoved the needle straight through. Then I didn't know how to secure the end, whether to take another stitch or what. I finally just pulled it tight and left it.

It would be nice to say the boy lived and the people cheered, "Viva." But the boy died that evening. I put my ear down to his mouth the last thing before going to bed. There was a faint scratching of breath, but his body was already starting to stiffen in death. Halsey's planes came too late for him. And the people did not cheer.

They were waiting for me when I came out of the hut to wash the blood off my arms. People from all over everywhere were there, the boy's wife, too. They had been afraid to come in to help because of the blood and the wound. Even the boy's wife had not had the strength to come in to help.

"He will not live," I told them.

I felt so very bad. But it is only in the storybooks that hard work, effort, trying, and trying again and again come out to have a happy ending. Working in the guerrilla had taught me that much.

"At least he will not have the mark of the Japanese on him when he goes to God," one said.

"He will have the mark of the American," he continued sorrowingly. "It is better to be before God with the mark of the American. It is the mark of love."

They were trying to comfort me, but the boy's wife kept sitting doubled over and crying into her hands because she had not had the strength to come in to help.

Then the planes came. Holy cow, there never was such a day anywhere before. I was just getting out of bed. There was a droning that filled the sky. The guerrillas must be getting very important, I thought, if the Japs send all that number of planes for us. The boys came running.

"Sir, planes," they cried, "planes, planes, planes, many, many planes, sir."

I ran to the clearing. We were sending plane flashes to MacArthur then and I wanted to count the flight and check its course. For a minute I couldn't take the sight in. My heart was in my eyes, I guess. Then I realized they were American planes. They were a type I had never seen before. After all, the last American planes I had seen had been nearly three years ago. But there was the star, there was the good old unmistakable star.

"American planes?" the boys cried.

"Why, of course," I said. "You don't think the Japs have that many planes, do you, and every one of them brand-new?"

I tried to be nonchalant. But gee, I couldn't keep a straight face at all, and pretty soon I was cheering my head off.

Those planes came over every hour on the hour all day long for three straight days. It was just incredible, that's all. We cheered ourselves into rags. They all came right over our clearing. Then, on the way back, they passed our clearing again. We clapped our hands sore. We jumped like balloons. We felt floating in the air.

The raid was on Manila. We saw only one example of bombing. There were 360 Japs coming on a lugger to relieve the garrison at Guyuan. The lugger had the bad luck to be offshore on the hour. Three planes dropped out of formation to have a look at it. Only one bombed. It hit square. Then he came back and dropped another. That hit square, too. Holy cow, if he'd have missed I'd have had some explaining to do, but as it was all I had to tell the Filipinos was, "What are you getting so excited about? American planes don't miss. They never miss."

What days, what days! Gosh, what jumpy days those were for the heart!

35

I don't know what effect the great September raid had on the other islands of the Philippines, but where I was it had this effect: the commanding officer of the BCs in the area came calling to see me. He walked directly up to a volunteer guard—whose identity was supposed to be secret—and said, "Please tell Major Richardson I would like to talk to him."

The volunteer guard was consternated. He ran off to alert an outpost I had established. The commanding officer—a lieutenant—waited patiently on the road. My boys in the outpost surrounded him and then advanced on him with guns.

"No, no, my comrades," he said, "put away your guns. I come to offer aid."

They led him to me with their guns in his back.

"You see," he told me, "I knew exactly where you were, and yet I did not bother you."

"I knew where you were and I did not bother you," I replied courteously.

This was true. The Samar guerrillas and I had discussed wiping out the BC garrison of thirty, but they had said the garrison would only be replaced by Japs and they preferred the BCs because police were lazier.

"You did not bother me except to steal my automobile generators," he laughed.

"They were stolen by you from the people; we took them back for the people."

"Well, I do not quarrel with you about generators. I have come to offer you my services and the services of my command, as was promised."

"By whom was it promised?"

226

"By us. When the Americans come, we leave the Japanese and join the Americans. That was the promise."

"By whom was it promised?"

He mentioned the name of a guerrilla leader. "And by us," he added. "We made the promise together."

I rolled a cigar. I did not offer him one.

"When the Americans come," I said finally, "we will kill you."

"No."

"Oh, yes, we make only one promise to traitors, that we will kill them."

There was a sound of machine-gun firing. I kept down the start in me.

"It was a promise," the lieutenant said wildly. Then he heard the firing and turned his face, frightened, towards the door.

There were two sets of machine guns firing now, and I could hear the airplane motors among them. People were running outside past the door. The lieutenant started to leave.

"I haven't given permission to go," I said.

"I was not going."

He drew himself up stiffly and stood stiffly while I fought down the fear in me and lifted the cigar to my lips and lit it. We could hear machine-gun bullets going into a house near us. Then a string of bullets picked at and kicked the dust outside the door. After that, it was over and we could hear the airplanes grinding lower and lower into the distance. Then the smell of burning drifted towards us.

"The house of Vidal is on fire," one of my boys reported. "There were two planes of the Hapons. A fire-making bullet hit a pillow in the house of Vidal, and now the whole house is burning."

They were cutting the brush to keep the fire from spreading.

"You see, the Americans have not won yet," said the lieutenant of police. "Our aid is not to be spurned."

"We do not take aid from traitors. From traitors we take only their lives."

"We are not traitors. We joined the BC only to

protect our people from the Japanese. The Japanese would have murdered many if not for us."

"You burned their houses."

"We were compelled. We had to be obeyed. It was either burn houses to make the people obey us or turn the people over to the Japanese. We preferred to burn empty houses."

"The houses were empty because you looted them, and then you burned them. It is true, I agree, you did not burn what you had stolen."

"We are not traitors. None in the BC is a traitor. We have all joined to protect our people from the Japanese."

"I do not care to argue."

"No," he cried.

"No, not argue," I said. "I will tell what I know to be true. Our airplanes opened your eyes. You saw them and they opened your eyes and when your eyes were opened you saw your own death before you. Then you came running, sniveling here that you have been a patriot all the time. You are a traitor. You cannot hide with words what you are. You are a traitor, and you will be killed for it."

"We come to fight Japanese."

"No, you don't. No sir, you don't. You came running away from the sight of your own death. If you wish to surrender, then surrender, not to offer to fight. Bring your men. Turn in your guns and their guns and I will have you taken to the guerrillas where you can surrender decently and honorably."

"Why should we surrender? We are not traitors."

I knew what he was afraid of. If he gave up his guns, he would be held for trial. He would be held behind barbed wire and there would be no chance to redeem himself before trial. If he joined the guerrillas, perhaps there would not even be a trial.

"We stood as defense between the Japanese and our people," he said. "We do not want to surrender our guns. We want to fight Japanese."

"Go lick a salt brick," I said.

Then a rather curious thing happened. The BC lieutenant went away, carrying his .32 pistol with him. A day later a Jap patrol came down the road from Hiporlos. They had heard of the BCs' desire to surrender, or perhaps they were just seeking to anticipate it. Perhaps all the BCs everywhere and all the fifth columnists and traitors and Jap spies and rats everywhere were jumping from the sinking ship at the first whiff, the first faint crackling of the fires of vengeance, and the Japs had known they would and were set for them. Anyway this Jap patrol, thirty of them, came to disarm the BCs, and the BCs laid an ambush for them.

It was a great pleasure to me.

Only twenty-five of the BCs had the guts to man the ambush. The other five ran away. There was a nice road-cut for the ambush. The BCs deployed in a seventy-five-yard line along both sides of the road-cut, figuring to shoot down into it. Then the Japs came along in a skirmish line three hundred yards long, the men about thirty feet apart. There was no way to fit them all into the road-cut. The BCs did the best they could. They fired when the leading Japs were in the road-cut. But everybody wanted a close-up shot. The Japs in the road-cut were only fifteen feet away, so everybody fired at them, and what happened was that eight or nine Japs were hit with all the bullets the BCs fired and the rest of the Japs didn't even smell powder.

Then the BCs discovered the mistake they had made deploying along both sides of the road-cut. What they should have done was bunch their force on the side farther from the beach and the Japs wouldn't have been able to split them up and they could have made an effective fighting retreat. As it was, they had sixteen men on one side and nine on the other, and they couldn't pull their force together. The Japs did exactly what they had been trained to do. They deployed on both sides of the road and then there were sporadic engagements in high grass and through the jungle all that day, and night, until the Japs withdrew the following morning.

The BCs didn't even get the rifles out of the deal. They had killed fourteen Japs, but the civilians had made off with the rifles and with the rifles of two BCs that had been killed, too.

Everybody wanted to get in the guerrillas now. Everybody was jumping on the MacArthur bandwagon. It seemed to be driving towards them like a fire engine with charging white horses, and they were grabbing ahold.

The lieutenant returned to ask if he could join us now; he had killed Japs.

"You may kill a thousand Japs," I said, "but if you do not surrender to the guerrillas we will kill you."

He departed shaking his head. He couldn't surrender. He knew his crimes were irredeemable. He had to hold on to his guns.

36

I had been waiting for MacArthur to come for a lifetime, it seemed, ever since we had taken him off Corregidor in our PT boats. I had worked for it and, although I suppose it isn't becoming for me to say it, I had suffered for it, too. I had dreamed of his coming. Those little "I shall return—MacArthur" wrappers on the soap and chocolate had gone twisting like burning ticker tape through my mind as I slept, and I had thought it would be this way: MacArthur's boys would come charging up the beach; we'd go charging down to the beach, hitting the Japs in the back; we'd meet among the dead bodies of the Japs; we'd shake hands. "Well, well, fancy meeting you here, it's a small world, after all." I'd wake up yearning. I'd still be feeling the clasp of an American hand around mine.

"General MacArthur, I presume."

"Major and Ensign Iliff David Richardson of the Filipino guerrilla army and United States Navy, I presume."

And we would be standing there on an island full of the same old bananas and the same old budbud and coconuts and tuba and belonging to the jungle and to nipa huts and to the wild pigs rooting in it and the deer barking in it and the pythons coiled up in it and the cockatoos screaming over it. But it wouldn't belong altogether to them any more. It would belong to history. What we had done among the pythons and deer and so forth would become part of history now and would no longer be an unknown heartbreak among smothering men on a forgotten island.

However, the way it happened was that it didn't happen that way.

History started for me in the usual way. My radio broke down altogether. It shouldn't have. It was brand-new. But it did. I guess it knew it was working for a guerrilla. This time, when it broke down, I just couldn't seem to get it started again. So, after a lot of this and that, I packed it up and started for another weather and radio station on the island. It took five solid days of hiking and a day of paddling upriver to get there. Fortunately, their set was just like mine. We checked part for part and finally found the trouble. One connection in the leader had become unsoldered. It looked solid, but when you pressed it down it came undone. It took about nine seconds to fix it. However, the trip wasn't a total exasperation. They had been about to go off the air for lack of spare parts. I, with my scrounging talents well developed after years of guerrilla work, had an ample supply with me.

There were two Americans at the station—Gordon Smith and Bill Richardson. They said they had brought some mail for me from home and had sent it down with a boy named Johnson.

"He'll probably miss you. He's on his way to Leyte. He'll be back in a month or two and then we'll send the mail down by runner."

"Maybe I will have it for Christmas."

"About then. If it comes earlier, we'll save it for you until then."

"You save it one minute longer than necessary and I'll come up here for it with my tommy gun."

It was the first mail I had received since Bataan. I had been sending letters home on the subs, but I hadn't got an answer and didn't know whether the letters were getting through. I found out later my letters home to my mother had been delivered by the FBI in person with a warning that if a word about them was breathed to anyone the letters would stop.

Then we started back down. We were in a nipa hut along the Samar coast when a typhoon hit. It was about five in the morning. We had seen the typhoon gathering and had helped the hut owner lash his home to palm trees with ropes, and had secured the radio equipment behind the chicken pen where it would be safe from falling coconuts and trees. Then, eight o'clock in the morning, the

232

wind and rain gathering force all the time, the house blew down. I jumped out into the wind to keep the house from falling on me, and the wind just kept me up in mid-air, then turned me around and threw me back onto the house.

But I wasn't hurt, just scratched a little and bruised. None of us was hurt getting out of the hut. The boys and myself made a deck of two coconut logs to keep the radio equipment out of the water, which was puddling higher all the time. The radio stuff was in tin boxes. It had come high class that way from Souwespac and all I had to do was wrap a raincoat around it. I had a spare raincoat and gave it to the woman there. She got under it with her baby and we stayed all day huddled up against the wreck of the hut, trying to use it as a windbreak. We were afraid to move. Trees and coconuts were crashing all around us. They were whirling through the air like tree-bursts of fragmentation bombs. The typhoon did not die out until very late that night. It killed all the man's goats and chickens, but it didn't hurt any of us.

The walking was rough after that. Trees and houses lay in the road. All the bridges were down. We had to ford every stream through currents that had to be fought like millstreams. I pushed too hard, but I wanted to get back on the air. My heart began to bubble again from overexertion. I told the squishing and squashing to shut up. I promised, if it would shut up, I would sleep for a week once we got on the air.

We arrived at our camp at two o'clock in the morning.

The wind had blown down part of the house. It had cracked the antenna wires, just blowing the trees between which they were strung apart until the wires split. Trees had fallen in such a way as to obstruct the free line of the antenna. They would all have to be cleared away.

"Brother," I told myself, "this is where we came in."

I was very disappointed. I had thought now the radio was fixed we'd be on the air with a snap of the wrist, no pain, no strain. I lay a long time listening to the squishing and squashing of my heart before falling asleep.

But my engineer had co-operated beautifully, as I found out when daylight came. He had rigged up two six-volt generators with a belt and pulley to make a twelve-volt generator. The four batteries were fully charged. We banged into those trees like they were confetti, and the next day we were on the air to Leyte. There was some traffic for Major Richardson, a message asking me to report to Commander Parsons before October 17 and if that were impossible to remain at my present station until Parsons called for me.

What the hell? I was still puzzling over the message when there were explosions like distant thunder. It was the American fleet. MacArthur was landing on Leyte, and here I was, forty miles away with a message to tie me down!

37

There is nothing in the regulations that says a commanding officer whose command is in good order and who himself is ailing cannot take a few days off as rest cure. I sent a night-running messenger to prepare a banca and crew. I didn't want any delays in my rest cure. Then five o'clock the next morning I started out on it. Donayre, Teodoro, and another of my boys, Faelnar, came along. They needed a rest, too.

"Sigi legi, ho!" Sigi legi is what the Filipinos say when they mean you'd better shake a leg and get on the ball, you old tramp you, or you'll be sorry.

The BCs had all run away from Balangigi. They had run to Major Smith to surrender. Boom, boom. MacArthur's guns were soft thunder in the distance. There were no Japs in Hiporlos. Where are all the dear little Japs? "They sit on the backs of their legs outside their garrisons waiting for planes to bomb the garrisons." The guerrillas had raised the American flag over the schoolhouse. We stopped to salute it. The town cheered.

"Why do you not put up the flag of the Philippines, too?" I asked.

"No. Sir, MacArthur is coming. It is for welcome him only, sir."

There was pushing in the crowd and whispering in Visayan—"What did he say?" "He said . . ." "Who said?" "He said . . . then we said . . ."

"Americans will be glad to see the Filipino flag, too," I declared.

A tremendous cheer broke from the crowd. There were screams of "What did he say?" mingled in it and screams of "He said . . ." and finally all understood what I had said and the cheers became so great they were like fists thrust into the ear.

The Filipino flag went up alongside the American flag. A man grabbed me. "Sir, please." He had been saving something three years for the liberation. Would I share it with him, please? It turned out to be three bottles of Coca-Cola, all dusted over like old wine. Hell, I thought, just when MacArthur has brought the whole of the United States here, that would be when I get this, instead of a year ago! The Cokes were warm, but they were good and had the taste of home in them.

Then we had to stay for lunch. We had monkey meat and rice. Monkey meat is meat all right, but you have to acquire a taste for it. It is so strong you have to boil out some of the taste of it before roasting. I had acquired the taste after we got enough bullets to waste a few hunting.

We got under way about one o'clock. We could make out the ships of the fleet on the horizon. They were just tiny baby shapes to us. Our banca's sail was of raffia. The wind was brisk and the sail tore and we had to tack back and get another one. By the time a cloth sail was rigged, the wind had died and we had to snail along sculling.

Every three minutes, the planes would pass overhead in threes and nines. They'd be testing their guns when they passed overhead or, if they were on the way back to their carriers, they'd be clearing them. I didn't have an American flag with me, but I waved everything I had. I wanted to make sure they understood the banca was not Jap, but was Ensign Richardson, U.S.N.R., leading Task Force Minus-Zero to reinforce MacArthur.

I tried to sing up a wind. It's a Filipino custom. You sing a few bars from a wordless, centuries-old, imploring kind of song. Then you wet your finger in the water and hold it up into the wind. If your finger gets cooler, the song is working. If singing does not work, you try whistling the same imploring song. The big thing is to stand aft of the mast and whistle right into the sail. If you get forward of the mast, the wind will blow backwards.

It worked. Anyway, something worked and a wind crept slowly up on us and we crept slowly along before it. It was then about four o'clock. At five o'clock we had chow—carabao meat and rice. We were still about ten miles from the ships. I couldn't see them firing. Their hulls were below the horizon. There were only three or four ships. I wondered what had happened to the rest of them.

Then at about six-thirty in the twilight, the sky suddenly became riddled with tracers. There were millions of them. I was startled. I saw the tracers before I heard any sound of gunfire, and then the sound rolled over the water steady and drumming. We kept making steadily for the battle. It was like old times. It was like Bataan days: no trouble about a course, just steady on where the gunfire is.

After the guns had stopped shooting, the wind died completely and we just sat where we were for a long time until suddenly there was a big ship gliding by near us. They had spotted us. They passed at about two hundred yards and winked a recognition signal at me. I was scared to death because I didn't know how to answer.

"I am Major Richardson," I bellowed. "I am going to Leyte. Request instructions."

The sleek, tranquil, powerful ship glided silently on and my heart sank.

Then I remembered I had given Teodoro a signal flashlight. I sent him scrambling for it on the double. It gave a nice, white light. I shone it on the water and flicked out in Morse code:

"I am an American officer en route to Leyte. Request instructions where to land. Major Richardson."

The destroyer was about six hundred yards off. It turned and came prowling back.

"Come alongside aft," a voice megaphoned.

We sculled like mad. We put our backs into it, and our hearts. The clouds slid away from the moon and the moon shone full on the destroyer. I saw that every gun aboard, including the main battery, was trained on us.

"I am Major Richardson," I cried, "an American guerrilla."

There was no answer. The guns remained trained.

I surrender, dear, I thought.

The destroyer was dead in the water. When we got

about thirty feet away, they told us to stay where we were. Sailors lined the rail looking down at us. A chief came among them.

"The condition is still red," he bellowed. "Get back to your battle stations.

"On the double," he bellowed. "On the double," and clapped his hands.

The crowd thinned out a little.

"Who are you?" It was the voice of an officer.

"I am Major Richardson, and I'm in the navy, too."

I heard someone say, "This guy is crazy."

"I am a guerilla." They didn't know what a guerrilla was, the Spanish way I pronounced it. "I am an American gorilla," I cried.

"He thinks he's Gargantua," someone said. "I told you the guy is crazy."

Finally the officer said to come alongside. I came bow on, because of the outriggers. *"Henay! Henay!"* I said to the boys sculling.

"He's talking Jap."

"No," I cried up to the ship. "That's Visayan. That's Filipino for slower, slower."

We bumped up gently against the ship.

"Stay where you are!"

The officer turned a flashlight on me. I had my sun helmet on, jungle boots, khaki shorts, khaki short-sleeved shirt with the major's insignia darned in by Curly. My pistol was in my belt and my tommy gun looped over my shoulder.

They threw me a line. Then they let down a rope ladder. The officer kept his flashlight on me while I scrambled up. There was a cable railing there and a big bosun's mate, about six feet three, grabbed hold of me and hauled me over it and held me while they frisked me of my guns. I just stood there grinning. I was tickled to death. I showed them my navy ring and my dog tags from Corregidor. I was grinning so much I couldn't talk. I just held them out.

They let my three boys come aboard the destroyer, and the banca crew shoved off to return to Samar. The boys were dressed in abacá shorts, all dirty and ragged, and wore no shoes.

"Is this the army?" cried a sailor. "Where's their clothes?"

Teodoro held up his trigger finger happily. "Sir, here is my uniform only."

They took me to the wardroom in officers' country and took my boys below. Chow was next on the menu for all of us. Good old American chow. I had been waiting three years. I could hardly wait another minute. They brought it on, steaming platters of it. I found I couldn't eat it. It was too rich for my taste after eating bamboo all that time.

"I guess I'm too excited to eat good," I explained apologetically.

They were all standing around watching me.

"Let's try this," suggested the skipper.

He shoved a cereal bowl piled high with ice cream at me. I didn't talk after that. I just put my head down and wolfed steadily. The skipper stood over me. When he saw I was nearly finished, he silently held up one finger to the messboy, meaning bring on one more bowl of ice cream. The messboy pushed the fresh bowl into place while I was still lifting the last spoonful to my mouth.

I started to laugh then. I couldn't help myself. Once I started, I couldn't stop. I laughed until there were tears in my eyes. Even then I couldn't stop. The tears rolled down my face, and still I couldn't stop.

"Hey," said the skipper, "your ice cream is melting."

That stopped me.

I took a shower in a real shower and bunked down in a real bed with springs and white sheets and a pillow. But I couldn't sleep. The bed was too soft. I finally finished up on the rug on the deck.

When I came topside in the morning, I saw three Filipino mess attendants. They were my boys! They had complete navy uniforms on—hats, dungarees, shirts, black shoes, everything. Under their arms, they each had about six cartons of cigarettes, bottles of hair oil, soap, shaving cream, razors, boxes of chocolate bars.

The crew had given them everything but the hull of the ship.

Subsequently I was ordered to the cruiser *Nashville*. Some colonels talked to me, passing the time of day sort of, while I wondered what the order had been about.

"The general will see you now, sir," said an orderly.

That still didn't register with me. I followed the orderly about fifty steps, turned in to a cabin, and there sat General Douglas MacArthur. I was stupefied. The general stood up and walked around the desk and held out his hand. I was so surprised I didn't even hold out mine. He had to take it from my side.

"General Kenney," he said, "this is Major Richardson."

I shook hands with General Kenney all right. I had recovered by that time. To our way of thinking, General Kenney is the greatest figure the air corps has produced.

Our talk lasted about ten minutes. I don't remember much about it. It consisted mostly of questions by General MacArthur. Hell, you don't just sit and shoot the breeze with a general. I remember feeling impressed and sort of humble in the presence of such important talent as MacArthur and Kenney and surprised to find out that not only had MacArthur read every single message we had ever sent out, but he seemed able to recall the detail in each of them. However, I remember mostly the feeling of pain I had every time I forgot to say "sir." The pain was quite frequent. I hadn't said "sir" to anybody in so long, I kept forgetting.

38

The greatest naval battle in history, the Battle of the Philippines, consisted for me just of watching gun flashes on the horizon and star shells and the orange-red glow of fires.

And I guess that about winds the story up. I worked with the army air corps awhile, helping them out on spotting Jap targets. We had quite a guerrilla reunion in Tacloban—Colonel Kangleon, Joe Rifareal, and myself. We hugged each other skinny. Then I helped out on liaison work between the army and the guerrillas.

That was funny. That was guerrilla business all over again. We had a pile of trouble making contact because the army radio sets were too good, too precise. The homemade guerrilla stuff was all coil-controlled instead of crystal and we could get on any frequency because we wandered all over the air. But with precision goods, we had to do plenty of nail-chewing.

Then orders came for me to return home for rest and reassignment. "You're in the navy now, Mr. Richardson, you son of a gun." I couldn't even get in on the fight for Malitbog. Chick Parsons took care of that with two U. S. Navy landing craft, infantry, and the guerrillas.

The guerrillas waited on both sides of the Casa and the LCIs came banging in from the bay. They caved in the whole front of the Casa and the Japs that were still alive ran out the back. About fourteen of them made it across the jai-alai court. The guerrillas had not been able to stay in back of the Casa because that's where the shells were landing.

However, the rest of the Japs holed up in dugouts in the patio. They had dugouts connected by tunnels. The guerrillas captured one, tied a rope around his neck and swung him down into a dugout to argue the rest into surrendering. They held the rope taut so that if the Japs down there started monkeying with it they would know about it. But the Japs didn't bother their comrade who had surrendered. They listened to him a long time and then sent him back to say no, they would stay where they were.

The Japs died there. The guerrillas blew them up with grenades and then caved in the dugout on top of them.

I didn't even get to see Curly again. I had to leave in a rush to catch my ship, and I sent her a message by Joe Rifareal. The message consisted of . . . well, it said mostly the word "darling."

ABOUT LT. RICHARDSON

LT. ILIFF DAVID RICHARDSON devoted the money allotted to his last two years in college to travel in Europe and the near and middle east. His travels appear to have been more educational than his two years at Compton College, for they taught him what college had not seemed able to —that there was going to be war, that it would be a world war and the United States would be in it. Richardson returned home to Los Angeles shortly before the fall of France in 1940 and enlisted in the Navy, asking for assignment to the Asiatic Squadron. He arrived in the Philippines aboard a mine-sweeper in the autumn of 1940, was transferred in 1941 to the famous expendable Motor Torpedo Boat Squadron 3 and fought torpedo boats until they were actually expended, doing odd murderous chores around Bataan, Corregidor, Cebu and Mindanao—striking against Jap warships, transports and landing barges, evacuating General MacArthur and staff. For performing these missions with "marked skill and coolness . . . in the face of greatly superior enemy forces," Lt. Richardson was awarded by General MacArthur the Army's Silver Star with oak leaf cluster in lieu of a second silver star and in addition wears the blue ribbon with oak leaf cluster representing two Presidential citations of the unit in which he served. When Corregidor fell and the last torpedo boat was sunk, Richardson declined to include himself out of the war. This book is the story of what happened to him afterwards.

ABOUT THE AUTHOR

IRA WOLFERT was the only reporter with the Free French at the liberation of St. Pierre and Miquelon. In 1942 and 1943, he accompanied our troops and reported on fighting in Guadalcanal (which earned him the Pulitzer Prize) and the Solomon Islands. During 1944, he landed in France on D-Day and junketed with the First and Third Armies through Normandy and the west of France. Mr. Wolfert is the author of several books of nonfiction, novels and short stories, including *Tucker's People*, *Torpedo Eight* and *Battle for the Solomons*.

BANTAM WAR BOOKS

Now there is a great new series of carefully selected books that together cover the full dramatic sweep of World War II heroism—viewed from all sides and representing all branches of armed service, whether on land, sea or in the air. All of the books are true stories of brave men and women. Most volumes are eyewitness accounts by those who fought in the conflict. Many of the books are already famous bestsellers.

Each book in this series contains a powerful fold-out full-color painting typifying the subject of the books; many have been specially commissioned. There are also specially commissioned identification illustrations of aircraft, weapons, vehicles, and other equipment, which accompany the text for greater understanding, plus specially commissioned maps and charts to explain unusual terrain, fighter plane tactics, and step-by-step progress of battles. Also included are carefully compiled indexes and bibliographies as an aid to further reading.

Here are the latest releases, all Bantam Books available wherever paperbacks are sold.

AS EAGLES SCREAMED by Donald Burgett

THE BIG SHOW by Pierre Clostermann

U-BOAT KILLER by Donald Macintyre

THE WHITE RABBIT by Bruce Marshall

THE ROAD PAST MANDALAY by John Masters

HORRIDO! by Raymond F. Toliver & Trevor J. Constable

COCKLESHELL HEROES by C. E. Lucas-Phillips

HELMET FOR MY PILLOW by Robert Leckie

THE COASTWATCHERS by Cmd. Eric A. Feldt

ESCORT COMMANDER by Terence Robertson

I FLEW FOR THE FÜHRER by Heinz Knoke

ENEMY COAST AHEAD by Guy Gibson

THE HUNDRED DAYS OF LT. MAC-HORTON by Ian MacHorton with Henry Maule

QUEEN OF THE FLAT-TOPS by Stanley Johnston

V-2 by Walter Dornberger

Bantam Book Catalog

Here's your up-to-the-minute listing of over 1,400 titles by your favorite authors.

This illustrated, large format catalog gives a description of each title. For your convenience, it is divided into categories in fiction and non-fiction—gothics, science fiction, westerns, mysteries, cookbooks, mysticism and occult, biographies, history, family living, health, psychology, art.

So don't delay—take advantage of this special opportunity to increase your reading pleasure.

Just send us your name and address and 50¢ (to help defray postage and handling costs).